EDDIE IRVINE

LIFE IN THE FAST LANE

EDDIE IRVINE

LIFE IN THE FAST LANE

The Inside Story of the Ferrari Years

With Jane Nottage

EBURY PRESS
LONDON

First published in Great Britain in 1999

10 9 8 7 6 5 4 3

© MSM Motorsport Management Ltd 1999

First published by
Ebury Press
Random House
20 Vauxhall Bridge Road
London SW1 2SA

Random House Australia (Pty) Limited
20 Alfred Street, Milsons Point
Sydney
New South Wales 2061, Australia

Random House New Zealand Limited
18 Poland Road, Glenfield, Auckland 10
New Zealand

Random House South Africa (Pty) Limited
Endulini, 5A Jubilee Road
Parktown 2193
South Africa

Random House UK Limited Reg. No. 954009

www.randomhouse.co.uk

A CIP catalogue record for this book is available from the British Library

ISBN 0-09-18746-02

Papers used by Ebury Press are natural, recyclable products made from wood grown in sustainable forests.

Designed and typeset by Behram Kapadia
Printed and bound in Great Britain by Biddles Ltd, www.Biddles.co.uk

CONTENTS

Foreword by Eddie Irvine

•••

1999 was an incredible year, my last year at Ferrari, my chance to go for the World Championship, a year lived on the edge of the precipice.

All four years at Ferrari have been an incredible experience. Michael Schumacher has an amazing natural talent, it just blows you away, and if you use your time with him wisely then you can learn and adapt your own style and then move on.

I'm glad I decided to write this book and set down on paper some of my thoughts and feelings about driving for Ferrari and also about my lifestyle. I consider myself to be a lucky man, I have a fantastic life, I have my own private jet, my own boat and all the toys a man could want. They call me the most toyed up driver in the Paddock and that's probably true, but no one can say I take it for granted. I love life and I love making the most of every moment.

I spend a lot of time on the boat with friends and family. It's my refuge and my home. When someone said 'What you need, when you have the money, is a boat' I thought 'I need a boat like I need a hole in the head,' but he was right, the boat is fantastic. I can relax on it without people staring at me or trying to make conversation, like you get at a hotel. Within five minutes of checking into a hotel everyone knows you're there. But I can float around on my vodka palace and no one knows what I am doing or who I'm with. When you lead the life I do, privacy is a valuable commodity.

As for the women – I like them. Most of my ex-girlfriends become friends when our relationship is over, and that's the way I like it, nice and balanced, no hassle. It's said that I don't respect women but that's rubbish. I love the company of women, I don't just go out with them for sex. The ones I get involved with, I get involved with because they are good company, a laugh and a giggle. Then there's my daughter Zoe who is mega, she is a great kid and I have a great situation with her. We spent lots of time together this year and it was great. I am lucky in that I have a great relationship with her mother, Maria. She is fantastic, she has handled the situation wonderfully, and we get on very well. The only difference of opinion we have is about where she and Zoe should live. We'll have to see who will win that one.

On the track, this year has been the best so far. When I got a chance to go for the World Championship, I grabbed it and it nearly came off. The boy from Newtownards could have been World Champion with Ferrari, but instead I'll just have to wait for Jaguar. Having had a taste of it I don't intend to give up. In fact I have a better chance with Jaguar than if I'd stayed at Ferrari, where Michael will be the number one again.

You can read about the Ferrari years and what it is like to race with the most powerful team in Formula One. Ferrari is like no other team, and that kind of power is incredible to experience. Will they make it in the future? Who knows? Personally, I don't think it's a good idea to put so many of your eggs in one basket with one driver. If you do that and something like Silverstone happens then it's difficult to pick up and run with the next guy.

There are things I'd like to change in F1. For instance, I think we should have two pit crews per team so each driver has the same advantage. I have many other views and you can read about them here in this book. You can also read about what my friends think of me. I've had a laugh reliving some of the things we've got up to during the last few years. My group of friends are a small band but we know how to enjoy ourselves and you can't ask for more than that.

If I had my time again I wouldn't change anything. I think I've made the right moves at the right time. I'd just change that last race and win the World Championship, but maybe that's for another time. You might think this is *Men Behaving Badly*, but if you got the chance to have my life would you do any different?

There have been many people who have helped with this book. My mum and dad, my sister Sonia. who is an angel, my manager Enrico, who is a friend as well as a business partner, Jane, who worked so hard on the book, everyone at Ebury Press and of course Ferrari, my racing colleagues, my friends, my lovers and most of all my lovely daughter, Zoe.

EDDIE IRVINE
NOVEMBER 1999

Introduction
by Jane Nottage

●●●

The chance to write Eddie Irvine's book on the Ferrari Years couldn't be passed up. Colourful, talented, outspoken, he stands out from the grey men who often inhabit the rarefied world of Formula One. In a sport where the commercial interests of both the sponsors and the media far outstrip the competitive interests of the sport, there are very few opportunities for heroes and villains to emerge. Teams try and keep their drivers under constant control. They indoctrinate them to say nothing controversial in case it offends the sponsors, to do nothing outrageous in case a stray photographer captures it on film and makes a quick buck from selling the image to a tabloid newspaper, above all never to disagree with the FIA (governing body). This would risk having to make an unexpected trip to Paris for a bit of wrist slapping, and the possibility of being given an enforced holiday.

If a driver can negotiate his way round this little maze he has his own team boss to fear. In some cases if you don't toe the party line, then you might not be driving for the team next year. In addition, drivers need to be at their peak of physical fitness to cope with the demands of driving round a modern grand prix circuit. Gone are the days when drivers of the old era would spend the night drinking champagne and bedding the most beautiful women, before rising at dawn to prepare for the race ahead. Today, most drivers are in bed with a mug of ovaltine and four rolls of telemetry print-out to study, rather than clutching a glass of Bollinger in one hand and a fun loving blonde in the other. There is, however, one exception. Eddie Irvine is still upholding some of the traditions of the old school of racing driver. That doesn't make him any less dedicated, but it makes him more of a character, and more of a challenge. You don't mess with Edmund. A lesson many journalists have learnt to their cost over the years.

The shadow of Eddie Irvine was present for many months before I actually met him. It was 1996 and I'd just started writing my Ferrari book, so I was doing the season. I joined the press pack and bounced around the world, from Brazil, to Argentina, to Imola, to Spain, to Britain, to Germany, to Italy and so on. The awesome Michael Schumacher had joined the team with Eddie Irvine as his number two. That fact made the Irishman hot property.

At various moments during the race weekend, journalists would stagger into the press room looking as though they'd gone a few rounds with Mike Tyson, or had just narrowly missed gunfire in a war zone. Pale and sweating, they'd reach for a cigarette with shaking hands, or down a strong coffee and mutter incoherently. After a few races, I established that the cause of such anguish was none other than the jovial looking Irish guy I sometimes saw at press conferences. 'He's a f******* nightmare to interview, won't answer questions, sits with his feet up reading a magazine, is monosyllabic, uncooperative, hates the press.' I decided the interview for the book could wait a while.

Eventually, it could wait no longer. By this time I was really puzzled. I'd met his sister Sonia who is his physio and manages part of his business life, and she is a really great person, very friendly and very approachable. She is also very good at her job and very dedicated even when under intense pressure. I'd also met his parents who are as well two of the nicest people you could hope to meet. How could he be such a sullen nightmare? Had he been accidentally swopped at birth? Was there a lovely guy with nightmare parents lurking somewhere in Northern Ireland? Or was he just suffering from an acute case of inflated ego disease, which is rather prevalent in Formula One?

On a summer's day in July at Silverstone I found out the truth. The nightmare wasn't a nightmare. It's just that Eddie Irvine doesn't take prisoners and patience isn't part of his character. He really does live life at 180 mph, and every minute counts. If you're unprepared or ponderous you're not given a second chance. Come in with well thought out, relevant questions and you'll always get a good answer. He's an intelligent and entertaining victim to interview.

Eddie Irvine is definitely a bit of an enigma. You never quite know what he is really thinking or what he is going to do next. He can change his mind a hundred times a day, declare he won't be going to the next PR event and then turn up, work hard and charm everyone. He'll chat on about various topics, related to racing or not, but very few people get to see the real Eddie Irvine. His manager, the smooth talking, energetic Enrico Zanarini sums him up well when he says 'He can talk for hours about nothing to girls who understand nothing.' And that's true, you can talk for hours without ever getting a glimpse of what really makes him tick. The best way to get to know the real Eddie Irvine is to observe the way he interacts with the people round him, his personality is reflected from those he's close to, and out it comes good and bad, sensitive and insensitive, instinctive and reflective.

During the following three years our paths occasionally crossed when I updated the Ferrari book. In May 1999 I went down to Monaco to interview Eddie for *Hello!* magazine. It was the day after the historic one-two Ferrari victory at Monaco, and the jet set town had sold more aspirins than Ferraris that day. Eddie was not in the mood for talk, and so the next layer of the Eddie Irvine personality was revealed. Leave him alone and he'll do the job in his own time, try and push him and you make an enemy. He likes laid back people, hates hasslers, and being told what to do and when to do it. You have to leave him to decide in his own time.

Then came the opportunity to write the book. I like a challenge and Eddie is definitely a challenge. What's more, it wasn't going to be the usual, blah, blah, blah, nothing interesting said type of book. 'Come down to the boat' they said. My heart sank. The last time on the boat in Monaco had been a nightmare – a hungover, irritable superstar and a heaving ocean, the combination of which was enough to make anyone want to lie down in a darkened room for a few days afterwards. Now, five days of being pitched around the ocean waves didn't sound like an ideal environment for some in-depth discussions on life on and off the track.

I set off with my seasick patches and it turned out to be a lot different from the first time. The superstar was as calm as the sea, and the interviews were full of typical intelligent Irvine observations and brilliant anecdotes. Anchored off Portofino with him and his family, including gorgeous daughter Zoe, was also a chance to get a glimpse of the real person behind the carefully contrived playboy, don't give a shit about anything image. Watching Eddie Irvine the father of Zoe, in action, was quite a revelation, and strange having seen and heard about Eddie Irvine the playboy. It was like observing two different people.

In spite of the love-them-and-leave-them attitude towards women, it was very clear that Maria is different. He respects her, likes her and enjoys being with her. You can't get to know someone after a few days, but having spent five days on the boat with Maria and Eddie's daughter, Zoe, it was very clear that she is a very special lady. Warm and caring towards her former lover, she also reads his moods and fits in with them on an almost instinctive basis. Brought up in the age of feminism, most western women demand equal rights in a relationship and are very vocal about getting attention when they want it. However, Maria has mastered the art of mixing submission with retaining a high level of self respect, and Eddie to his credit clearly recognises her qualities and how well her personality fits in with his mercurial, independent character. There was a relaxed, softer air about the man when he was with Maria and Zoe, and they could easily be the rock on which he could fix his anchor. The only impediment to that scenario is his restless desire to roam and seduce. Like some latter day Roman emperor he feels the day isn't complete without a bit of rape and pillage, or at least the latest model in his bed and a few Red Bulls and vodkas in his stomach.

But is the quick fix adrenalin high of chasing and bedding a new woman a match for the emotional peace of being with your soul mate? Only he can answer that question, and I think that deep down when he is alone, which he rarely chooses to be these days, he must wrestle with that problem. It's not easy to reconcile living life as though you're one of the stars of *Men Behaving Badly*, and living it as a father and live-in lover.

But there is no doubt that Maria has been a very important part of his life, and as the mother of his child continues to be. She adores his family and they adore her and little Zoe. But even apart from Zoe's presence there is something in Maria that Eddie recognises as right for him, and I think that in a few years' time, he might just regret letting her go. There aren't that many people who are right for each other, and Maria and Eddie just seem to be a perfect match. If she's good for him, then he is equally good for her, bringing excitement and unpredictability into her life, and also a fairly large dose of vulnerability, which she can deal with and get the satisfaction of knowing how to calm him and keep him on his toes in equal doses.

Even he has said that the most beautiful girl in the world can become ugly if she has an unattractive personality. Unlike many of the women Eddie meets, Maria isn't in love with the ritzy, glitzy package of Formula One star, the private jet, the boat, the boy's toys. She seems to genuinely love the man and accept the whole package, warts and all. For a man who, although very good looking and charismatic, is essentially shy and insecure, it must have been unsettling to have woken up next to a woman and know that if he was Eddie Irvine, Irish lad about town, rather than Eddie Irvine superstar, she probably wouldn't look twice at him, let alone be in his bed.

Maybe that is why he so values the comfort and love of Maria. There is also Zoe, and contrary to his own doubts, he has slipped easily into the role of father. Once again, Maria's attitude has facilitated the close rapport that has developed between father and daughter. As I know in my own case, the relationship between a father and daughter is unique, a combination of protector, guide, playmate and teacher, and I was surprised by how genuine the affection is between Eddie and Zoe. She is a delightful, happy child, and very easy to like, but even so Eddie Irvine playing with his daughter and patiently taking her round on the jet ski was not necessarily the most obvious image one would have of him.

He clearly enjoys every moment he spends with Zoe, and the relationship has developed into mutual trust and affection over the summer of 1999 when he spent time with his daughter. He makes it work, as he makes everything work. In fact that is one of the main strengths of the man. He makes everything work. Business, racing, personal relationships, he has the knack of making it all seem easy, and of co-existing with the most complicated situations, and keeping them all both integrated and apart. I can also see why he is attracted to his Dutch model girlfriend Anouk. She is beautiful, feisty and bright, and has won his respect as well as his love. Her fierce independence and honesty has ensured she's captured his head as well as his heart. I wouldn't be surprised if she's the one who stays the course. He rarely falls out with his girlfriends, and when they are no longer lovers they will often become friends, even if not in the same way that Maria and Zoe have captured his heart.

However, just because Eddie Irvine makes the juggling act look easy, doesn't mean that the man from Newtownards is easy. Complex and multi-faceted, he has a short attention span, and gets bored very easily. At 33 he's at his physical prime, fit and strong; emotionally, he's probably just passing adolescence; and intellectually he's very bright. He'll grab the meaning of complicated concepts and store information to regurgitate it at the relevant moment months or maybe years later.

One of the first things you get to know about Eddie Irvine is that he is composed of a vast number of seemingly contradictory characteristics. He is known as the number two driver with the number one mouth, yet this year he has shown skill and maturity in taking over the role of number one at Ferrari, with all the attendant pressures that brings. He kept the World Championship alive, while the number one driver Michael Schumacher recovered from a broken leg, and he matched his number one driver by taking the World Championship down to the last race, only to be outdone by the superiority of the McLaren car.

He may have missed out on the Drivers' Championship, but he made a large contribution to bringing the Constructors' Championship home, for the first time since 1983, and that is something to be very proud of.

Being Michael Schumacher's team mate could have been a recipe for disaster for Eddie. Michael is undoubtedly the best driver, blessed with unbelievable natural talent, and that isn't easy to live with. A lot of Schumacher's team mates seem to have felt crushed by the pressure of driving with the best in the world. And Michael, rightly so considering his talent, relishes his lead position. Until you're in the team, you can never realise just how important Team Schumacher is to Ferrari. The German race is known for its propensity for getting the best sunbathing spots round the swimming pool, and the beach towels are set out for Michael before the season begins and then kept in place throughout it. To try and secure your little part in the sun you need tenacity and a strong, balanced mind. Irvine has both even though he likes to hide behind the 'shag them and leave them' playboy philosophy.

Irvine has chosen a career that means he is constantly in the spotlight, yet he hates getting attention, and has an almost pathological dislike of being gawped at. In fact, apart from his talent as a Formula One driver, hiding is what he's really good at. On his boat, the Anaconda, he can hide with friends and family and be himself; in Dublin people tend to leave him alone to get on with life; on his private jet he has his own space. He doesn't like people getting beneath the surface. It's much easier to present an image, let people think he's the good time boy. But get below the surface and there's an interesting story to tell.

Eddie Irvine is one of the few drivers to improve his position in the Drivers' Championship each year. From finishing tenth at the end of the 1996 season, he fought for the World Championship in 1999, and only lost out by two points, coming an impressive second.

I think his straightforward, tell-it-like-it-is comments on his racing years at Ferrari make fascinating reading. How has he coped with the Schumacher factor? Is it good policy to have a team so dominated by one driver? What is Michael Schumacher really like as a driver and a person? What is it like in the inner sanctum of Ferrari? Who are the men at the top in Ferrari? Who makes the decisions and pulls the strings? How well do all the drivers get on with each other? What are the politics of the sport? Is the GPDA useful? Is the FIA (governing body) necessary? What really happened at Silverstone? How did Ferrari deal with Eddie's Championship bid?

Eddie Irvine is one of the sport's most fascinating characters and he is one of the few Grand Prix drivers with a story to tell. Four years with one of the most glamorous and enigmatic teams in Formula One is an experience most top racing drivers never have. He also has the lifestyle that goes with the job, endless beautiful women, parties and a nursery full of expensive toys.

Above all, he is very honest about his views, without whining. He never denied that Michael Schumacher is the best driver, while at the same time giving an insight into how the team is geared to the German driver's needs, sometimes, in Eddie's opinion, to its detriment.

It isn't easy to make a team out of so many different characters, and in Ferrari the characteristics of the various nationalities are very exaggerated. Team Boss Jean Todt is in a no-win position. Things go wrong, he gets blamed, things go right, it's the brilliance of the team. He is the man for whom the word stressed was invented. Fortunately, he is also extremely French, and his very Frenchness, that suspicion of the outside world, and the ability to instinctively know the political moods of his environment, has ensured his survival.

Ferrari Chairman, Luca di Montezemolo, is a brilliant frontman, the right man in the right place to promote Ferrari on an international basis. He is also quintessentially Italian, and the style and glamour he injects into his job ensure that Ferrari will always be at the forefront of the sporting world, and also a leader in the road car sector. But he wants results, and his patience could run out. Michael will have to deliver next year, and being very German he will probably just get on with the job and not allow any distractions. He has the single minded determination of the German population mixed with exceptional natural talent, and given the right car he will bring the Championship back to Maranello.

However, there is one element that in my opinion Ferrari will miss and that is the Irishness of Eddie Irvine. The Irish have the natural gift of bringing a bit of sparkle into the greyness of the world; they are irrelevant and humorous, illogical to the point of distraction, but still a welcome presence at any party. Ferrari will seem a little duller without the designer-clad playboy strolling through the doors shouting 'Yo, what's happening?' and making his way to the factory floor to see what the latest innovations are. He may not have brought the title to the stable of the Prancing Horse, but he was mentally strong and talented enough to keep Michael on his toes and offer real competition. He was also very popular, the ideal man for the fans to relate to.

A lot of the rich and famous moan constantly about their lot in life. What is so refreshing about Eddie is his sheer joy at his good fortune in life. He loves his toys, he loves the lifestyle and he loves the money. You get the impression that he wakes up every morning, grabs the guitar and starts playing 'Lucky Man'. Because that is what he is; sure, he has talent but a lot of people have talent, and as Eddie knows you need a little bit of luck and a large dose of determination to turn your dreams into reality.

A greater insight is given into Eddie Irvine through the eyes of his friends and family. Sonia is his sister, but also works with him. How does that work? Is it difficult to have your brother as your boss, particularly when you are the older sibling, and the one who used to protect your younger brother and make sure he was organised?

Sonia is an absolute key to Eddie Irvine Inc. She knows him better than anyone else, apart from his parents, and she ensures his life runs like clockwork, both at the track where she is in charge of every aspect of his life from diet, to physio, to making sure he is on time for meetings, to generating and co-ordinating his business activities. But what about her life? Is there life after Eddie Irvine Inc? How does she cope with his tantrums? After all, as she is one of the few people with the courage to say what she really thinks, she is often in the firing line of his verbal bullets.

His parents Edmund and Kathleen are also his greatest supporters. They travel to the races, happily living in their top-of-the-range camper van, where they have total freedom to go wherever they like and meet the many friends they have made round the world. Like Sonia they know the right balance of giving Eddie support and giving him space, also like Sonia they are his best PR, making time for the fans and representing Eddie Irvine Inc. They also know the real Eddie Irvine, the one the rest of the world doesn't know. You can read their views and insights into their son, and understand how his background has contributed to his gritty, determined character.

Enrico Zanarini is more than a manager. He is also Eddie's friend and a fellow party animal. They make an ideal team. Doing business, looking after sponsors, and then celebrating the success. If Eddie is hard and aggressive in his dealings with people, Enrico is the diplomat, the man with the patience to see the deals to conclusion. Enrico has his own perspective on life at Ferrari and life after Ferrari. He's the man who does the deals and his view on Eddie is fascinating reading.

Then there are the girls. What do they think of him? Anouk gives her views on the man she loves. Maria, the mother of his child, gives her insight into the man who is the father of her much loved daughter, Zoe. Other girls have loved and lost him, including some famous ones...

Hopefully, this is more than just a book about a racing driver, it is a book about a certain way of life, a lifestyle that is a cross between James Bond and Desperate Dan. Most men aspire to have the money and the energy to buy a lot of expensive toys and jet set round the world playing in the international hotspots, with unlimited access to beautiful women and with a small pack of loyal friends by their sides. Here is the man who lives that life. This is his story and the story of the people who have got close to him. It was a tough project to do in a very short time so there were plenty of tense moments, but in the end I was up at 5 am and really rooting for Eddie Irvine to win the Championship. He is the kind of character who causes mayhem and disagreement, but in the end he was the one man who should have been World Champion. It would have made the fantastic ending to the season, and would have brought a touch of colour and life to a sport that is too often grey and dull. Never mind, I'm sure there will be a next time for the man from Northern Ireland to win the ultimate dream prize, and when he does he'll richly deserve it.

JANE NOTTAGE
NOVEMBER 1999

CHAPTER 1

Australia

Sunday, 7 March 1999. Melbourne, Australia. Victory. I'd wanted this for so long and when it happened, it was even better than I'd imagined. It was a fantastic feeling to be standing on the top step of the podium and looking down at the sea of people below. In amongst the hundreds of faces I could see my race engineer, Luca Baldisserri, my mechanics and my sister Sonia. It gave me a real kick and incredible satisfaction to know that my side of the team had finally made it to victory.

Winning gives you the best adrenaline rush, but this victory also felt like a huge weight off my shoulders. What's more, I thought it had been achieved in the best way possible. I drove well, the car was great and every-thing went to plan. I qualified sixth but wasted no time in moving up to third at the start and I took second position when Coulthard stopped on lap 14. At one point I had had to back off from Hakkinen and was a sitting duck to be overtaken, but no other driver was alert enough to take the opportunity. My luck held and when Mika Hakkinen went out on lap 21, I was leading the race.

The second safety car was a potential problem as I'd pushed hard to distance myself from Frentzen. I was get-ting close to my pit stop, so it was vital that I opened up the gap again. Here the car came into its own and incredi-bly I was able to push it as hard as I had done in qualify-ing. I found myself thinking that this was finally the car that could do it this year, if we could just get it up to speed. After years of frustration, it was a fantastic change to get into a car and think 'This is a good base from which to work.'

Maybe the key to the whole weekend was the fact that

I'd done my own thing in terms of set up, which is the fine tuning of all the various elements – aerodynamics, mechanics, tyres and so on – to get the best possible combination for the car. I always want it set up to be easy to drive and fast. I'd only had a day and a half's testing before the Melbourne race, but I managed to work hard with Luca Baldisserri to get the car as I wanted it rather than how Michael Schumacher had left it. In that short time I got to know the car and started to work on the set up that would suit me. For the race I chose soft tyres, unlike most of the front runners, and that gave me a great start.

Strangely enough, I'd had a couple of phone calls from friends who said they'd had dreams predicting I'd win in Australia. Maria, my ex-girlfriend and mother of my daughter, Zoe, had called me to say she'd dreamt I'd win, and my friend Shiga, who lives in Japan, also called me to say he'd had a dream I'd win. I guess it just had to happen.

To win in a Ferrari was also very special. The ultimate triumph. Having been accused of being a playboy and of only wanting to go out and have fun, it was especially satisfying also to prove that you don't have to be a killjoy to win. Now, I hope, the young drivers out there can see you can win and still have fun. Life is about enjoying yourself. You can be deadly serious about the job in hand, as I am, and still party till dawn when success comes along.

Of course my old boss Eddie Jordan wasn't shy in coming forward and offering his congratulations after the race. He gate-crashed the Ferrari party and we exchanged a bit of banter. He always insists he's made me the driver I am today, and I have to admit it was he who gave me my chance in Formula One. Eddie's a very astute guy – he has made a fortune spotting talent and then getting other teams to pay a lot of money to buy the driver out of his contract. But all credit to him, he knows what Formula One is all about and can still have fun and party with the best of us. My two years at Jordan gave me a good lesson in how to get around Formula One, get the best out of it, and still enjoy myself.

Ferrari was in fact one of Eddie Jordan's biggest sponsors back in 1995 when they had to pay him off to get me. Jordan are like family to me, so when the initial fuss had died down after my win, I went and found Ian Phillips, the Commercial Director of Jordan, who is one of my best friends in motor racing, and we carried on partying. It was a mega party night. My manager, Enrico Zanarini, and I had a fantastic time. We got back to the hotel room at about five o'clock in the afternoon, Australian time, and found our rooms full of champagne. Everyone had sent bottles, so we just got stuck in. Before the season we'd worked out our strategy for the year, and a few bottles in, it suddenly struck us and we just looked at each other and said 'We got it right, didn't we?'

Five bottles later, we hit the casino and then the restaurant. We had the usual stunning girls and party people with us, who seem to form a posse around any event, and I eventually got to bed at about five in the morning. Enrico staggered back at eleven in the morning. Quite frankly, I don't know where he gets his energy from. The guy's in his mid-forties and he never stops. I sometimes worry about getting older, hitting forty and so on, but then Enrico says to me 'Thirty was better than twenty, forty was better than thirty, forty-five was even better, and forty-seven is better than that.' I guess as he's managing a Ferrari driver his career is as busy as it's ever going to be, but he still looks great and has endless energy. Looking at him it makes me think that however good my life is now, perhaps the best is still to come.

For now, though, I was happy to enjoy the moment and to be sharing it with those who had made it possible. When I moved from Jordan to Ferrari, my sister Sonia had become part of my business life and part of the Ferrari team looking after my diet and physio requirements. She also deals with the sponsors and with looking after some of my commercial interests. Happily she was there to help me celebrate in Australia. For all of us it was an emotional moment.

SONIA IRVINE

I was so proud of him. I was thinking 'It's finally happened! We've waited so long for this and here it is. I was crying when he was on the podium as the emotion hit me. My kid brother had won a Formula One race! So many people had worked hard for this moment and finally it had all come together.

Unfortunately my parents, Edmund Senior and Kathleen, were not with me for my first win. Sadly, my grandmother had died a couple of weeks before the race. She was my last grandparent so it was the end of an era. I was very close to her as she lived right outside our garage business and two hundred yards from our house. It was strange that a short time after one of the saddest moments of my life, I would be on a high and experiencing a dream come true in

Australia. But life is like that, or rather my life is like that, and I think the only way is to live life to the full and make the most of every moment. Even if they couldn't make it, my parents were watching the race.

Edmund Irvine Senior

It was all organised for us to go and watch the race, but when my mother died a couple of weeks before, we didn't feel like going. So Kathleen and I switched the telly on and watched it in bed. I thought Edmund had a real chance when he went into the lead but I have to admit I was very nervous watching it as I was worried the car would break down. People started to ring us before the end and we had to get them off the phone so we could watch the final moments. Also, we didn't want to celebrate until Edmund had taken the chequered flag. Once he crossed the line Kathleen and I went crazy, and the phones went crazy. We got up and partied all day into the next morning. That was a really good day. Any excuse for a party!

Like father, like son! Some things really do run in the family. However, although we were celebrating there were a few hard truths that had to be faced. We were all shocked when we arrived in Australia to find we were over a second off the pace in comparison to the McLarens. We had expected to be a little bit off the pace, maybe half a second, but to find it was over a second knocked our confidence a bit. We really thought we'd got it right this year. Although both McLarens subsequently went out of the race, and we realised they had speed but had compromised on reliability, well over a second is still a lot in Formula One terms. If they managed to get the reliability sorted out in the five weeks before we went to Brazil, we'd be in deep trouble.

I knew that the 1999 Ferrari was the best car we'd had. Ferrari Chief Designer Rory Byrne's first car for the 1998 season, although an improvement on previous models, hadn't quite lived up to expectations, but this year it just all came together and he produced a really great car. It should have been easy for us to get on with the job and leave the opposition standing, but that was before Adrian Newey was brought into the equation. When Newey went from Williams to McLaren it made it that much more difficult for everyone else. McLaren have more resources than Williams, and are probably slightly better organised as well. Now that they had the best aerodynamicist in the sport it got even harder to beat them.

Michael Schumacher came to Ferrari as the best driver in the world. He'd just won the World Championship twice and everyone assumed he was just going to deliver the title to Ferrari. The attitude was 'Oh well, if not this year then within three years Michael will be World Champion.' Not as long as Adrian Newey's around. The guy's brilliant, the best there is and I'd love to drive a car designed by him. For Ferrari to have a chance at the World Championship we need Newey to retire for a year or two. Maybe we could all have a whip round and pay for him to go on an extended holiday round the world. He could come back in, say, three years and see if he could still work his magic and win again. My bet is that he'd come back and clean up once more. There's no better aerodynamicist in Formula One.

Ferrari and McLaren seem to have completely different views of how to build a car. McLaren go for as much speed as possible and then work on reliability, and as my manager Enrico Zanarini puts it, Ferrari make a tank and then try and speed it up. To be quite honest I don't know which method is better as we usually arrive at the last race fighting neck-and-neck for the Championship. At least on this occasion in Melbourne the tortoise had beaten the hare. As well as the concerns about the McLaren speed lead, there was also a general feeling in the team that we were at a bit of a disadvantage with the Bridgestone tyres as most of our winter testing had been done on high grip circuits such as Mugello.

I also felt that Ferrari had been expecting Michael Schumacher to win. I sensed a slight feeling of lost opportunity within the team, which took the edge off the win. To be fair, it's always the same – if David Coulthard wins then Mika Hakkinen's mechanics will be hacked off. Ferrari is a one-man band. Everything revolves around Michael Schumacher and the whole team is designed for him to be the number one and win races. When the number two wins, it puts everything out of gear. Michael said he was pleased with my win and everyone said what a shame it was for Michael. My view is we're all in it for ourselves. There is no more selfish sport than Formula One. I think drivers put themselves before the team. Ultimately I'm in it for myself, not Ferrari. That's what it's all about. However, that doesn't mean to say that when the chips are down, you can't pull through for a team-mate. Michael's support for me, later on in the season, at the Malaysian Grand Prix, was incredible. When I really needed him, he was there and you can't ask for more than that. It takes real courage for the best driver in the world to help someone else win. Actually, it was back in Australia that I thought I was in with a chance to go for the World Championship, as you never know what the future holds. Look what happened to Damon Hill in 1994 when he went head to head with Michael.

Of course there was the usual carry-on of teams accusing other teams of having parts on the car which did not comply with FIA rules. We were accused of running with a flexible rear wing, which reduces drag and increases straight line speed. The real power brokers are Ferrari and Bernie Ecclestone. In my experience, Ferrari, the glamour boys of Formula One, has more power than all the other teams put together. As a team it is very effective in getting its voice heard about the design rules, the testing rules, everything.

Bernie is the one we need. He's a genius, incredible. Maybe he gets too much of the pie now, but without him Formula One wouldn't be anything like where it is. I hope he can stay around for another thirty years. He's irreplaceable. Without Bernie at the helm there would be a lot of infighting, and a lot of indecision and lack of foresight. You just have to look at how the teams react without Bernie. They were given the responsibility themselves to cut down on testing and what have they achieved? Nothing. With one tyre manufacturer in Formula One, we're not even having to push one competitor against the other as far as tyres are concerned, but we're still managing to spend more time testing with less to test. That's some achievement! Just going round and round doing nothing in particular testing something for no particular reason. That just shows you what the teams achieve without Bernie's input.

If I could change anything within Formula One, I would cut the testing schedule right down, it's a total waste of the world's resources. I would also limit the amount of money spent on engine development. There's too much money being sloshed about. If you limited the amount of money spent it wouldn't change who won, you'd still get McLaren in the lead because they have Adrian Newey. But some of the smaller teams would do well. Jordan doesn't have the budget that McLaren or Ferrari have but they are doing a blinding job because they have bloody good people.

Australia was the realisation of everything I'd worked for, but the story was only just beginning. I didn't realise what the rest of the year would bring, although my contract was up at the end of 1999, and as I wanted to take a lead role in a team, I was pretty sure I wouldn't be driving for Ferrari in 2000. Clearly the status issue there was not going to go away. I had had serious talks with Honda at the end of 1998, and had discussed terms. They were going to do what Jaguar are planning to do now, and run their own team. It was going to be mega. This was very much something I wanted to be part of. Also I have a good level of popularity in Japan due to my Formula 3000 days, and the idea of linking up with Honda was very attractive from that point of view. I believed they were going full steam ahead and I knew they had already got a lot of good people on board, and were getting a lot more. With my faith in the Japanese ability to build engines, I was convinced this was the way for me to go.

However, when the Honda team boss Harvey

Postlethwaite died, the project was put back. They decided to go with Reynard and BAR, which I thought was the wrong way to proceed. It was a halfway house, as if they were just engine suppliers. What's more it wasn't going to be their own team, so they would not get the publicity that was the whole point of the exercise for them. I think it would have been much better if they'd done their own thing. I said I'd go to Honda if they could get it together but as it gradually started to unfold I needed to look around again.

I was still talking to Ferrari, as I would continue to do until just after Silverstone, when they told me my services wouldn't be required for 2000. Ferrari were talking to every driver under the sun, as they do all the time. It's always like that in Formula One, everyone keeps their options open until someone makes a definite move and then everyone else falls into place. It's not unlike musical chairs, with some people getting the seats they want, some having to compromise and someone usually getting left out.

At least I took off in the jet from Australia leading the World Championship and whatever else was going to happen, I knew it was going to be an interesting year. The car felt good, and I was on a high. If I could get a few more chances at winning, I knew I could take them and make it work.

The F399 is an evolution of the 1998 car, so we've managed the reliability factor, whereas McLaren have a very new car. We're never quite sure exactly what they have in terms of horse power. They seem to be better on efficiency but I don't know whether their drivability is as good or worse than ours. Our 1999 car is lighter, and Rory Byrne has tried to make it more aerodynamically efficient. As usual we had an all singing, all dancing launch for the car with the standard promises to win the World Championship. We looked at the lessons of 1998 and realised that we had to be competitive at the beginning. As Michael said at the launch, 'We did not lose the title race in Japan, we lost it in the first five races. I cannot win the Championship if I am not able to compete properly in the first five grands prix.'

So, what happened? We went to Australia and found to our horror that we were over a second off the pace of the McLarens. Maybe not too good a sign that we were going to get stuck in at the beginning. The advantage we do have is that we have Ross Brawn, Ferrari's Technical Director, who is a very steady, 'Let's not panic' type of guy, which is absolutely vital at a team like Ferrari. Ross works methodically and will not be pushed into making changes for the sake of it. We can have worked on modifications for months, but if he doesn't feel they will make a significant difference then we don't put them on the car.

I think things really started to turn around at Ferrari when Ross joined at the end of 1996. That first year was a nightmare for me, when I went to Ferrari I didn't quite realise quite how geared the whole thing was to Schumacher as the number one driver. I certainly don't criticise Michael for that, but I totally underestimated how much the whole team was going to be focused on Michael Schumacher. It seemed to me that every department was going to be structured towards him, not only in racing, but even down to hotel rooms and cars. For example, there are tolls on many motorways in Italy, but you can get electronic toll passes that allow you to go straight through the barriers. Michael's road car had one of these telepasses and my car didn't. It was like the first and second division the whole time. To be honest I hadn't been hot for the Ferrari drive at the end of 1995, I'd been hot for Williams, but Ferrari was the way to get out of Jordan. At that time Jordan didn't have the money to make a winning team, and I wanted to win.

However, once I was there I knew I just had to get on with it and make it work which, as I've explained, is pretty much my philosophy in life. There was no point in trying to change things, or stamping my feet, I just had to work hard, get the best results possible and try to make progress. In 1996 I thought to myself, this has got to get better, which turned out to be correct. It wasn't too difficult to spot because of the investment Ferrari had made in Michael. If Michael hadn't been at Ferrari, Ross Brawn probably wouldn't have come, and Rory probably wouldn't have joined the team, either. They had to produce a car that would make Michael win as they knew they had an outstanding driver. I don't think that would have been the case if there'd just been two ordinary drivers at Ferrari. I remember John Barnard, Ferrari's ex-Chief Designer, saying that when Schumacher arrived, it was like another piggy bank had been opened, and that the money just flowed and flowed to make sure they got it right.

I managed to settle in to working in Italy and being part of Ferrari, and my results improved. In the end I think my success led to Ferrari deciding not to renew my contract at the end of 1999, but for the time being the first year was a baptism of fire. I had no choice, if I didn't make the best of it then I would be out on my arse. At the end of every year I always got offers from other teams, especially Jordan, but in the end I wanted to make it work at Ferrari. I just needed to create a bit of space for myself in the Schumacher machine and chalk up some decent results.

In the first year I had nine retirements in a row and I sat on the beach in Dublin while Michael did all the testing. I got increasingly lost and the car was breaking more and more. There was nothing I could do except sit it out and wait for an opportunity to make progress. The beginning of the year got off to a reasonable start in Australia. I qualified ahead of Michael and finished third. But that was the first and last good result. After that my qualifying went down the pan. Whereas at Jordan I could get out of the car and feel I'd really rung its neck and got the best out of it, I couldn't do that with the Ferrari. It was good in the cold and awful when it was warm. It would have been fine if we'd had grands prix in Alaska, but it wasn't much good in the heat of South America or in the European summer.

My problem was I just didn't understand why I couldn't get the best out of it even if it wasn't a great car. I just didn't have the confidence to brake late for some reason and so I qualified very, very badly. I recall thinking 'Jesus, there's no way this car should be back here.' It was very depressing.

My worst qualifying was a second and a half off Michael and when I had a good day in 1996 and 1997 I could run within four or five tenths off him. I still felt I could go better than that. In the Jordan car every other qualifying session I'd think 'Jeez, that was good.' Every other race I'd be in the top six, which in a Jordan at that time was very good, because it wasn't one of the top cars. My average over Barrichello was something like six or seven tenths, so I needed to understand at that stage what the problem might be.

Michael was doing a lot better. In spite of the mechanical failures, he still won three times in Spain, Spa and Monza. He did have a massive advantage, however, in having the team structured round him. A lot of people don't understand what that really means. They think 'Sure he had the best engine and tyres and the spare car and most of the testing, but that doesn't mean the number two should be that much off the pace' but it extends beyond that.

But I have to say that in my opinion the way Ferrari is structured didn't just affect my morale, it can also potentially be bad for team morale.

I have a good relationship with Ferrari Chairman Luca di Montezemolo – I'm straightforward with him and he knows that. I don't try and cover anything up, and I don't try and pretend things are different to what they are.

Michael is undoubtedly the best driver in the world, I've never denied that and it's been a great experience working with him. Put simply, the guy's a genius on the track. He has an enormous dose of natural talent which means he can just drive through problems and get the best out of a fairly mediocre car. I've taken the best bits of Michael and tried to use them in my own driving style. I've tried to go into corners in a smoother, faster way and take on other aspects of his driving skill as well. He knows where the limit is and is on it as soon as he's in the car. That's a pretty rare ability. But driving with Michael

Schumacher can also have a negative effect. You see the times he's doing and you think 'Shit, I've got to push really hard to do that time.' Sometimes, though, you actually don't have to push hard. In fact, my times have always ended up lower when I've tried too hard. When I just drive and give the car its head, then it all comes together much better than if I try and force it to go as fast as possible. You have to take it easy, smooth it all out and let it happen.

Maybe the problem is aiming at a number. You see Michael's times and you think 'I've got to aim for that,' when really you should be aiming to be half a second off. Perhaps aiming for a number has a bad effect on the driver. If you look at the effect Michael's had on other drivers, it reinforces the point. Johnny Herbert for example, was good in all the formulas coming up and he was quicker than Hakkinen when they were at Lotus. Brundle did a fantastic job at Jordan in 1996, and yet these guys were nowhere compared to Michael and they were actually qualifying worse when they were with Michael than they should have been. He's a hard act to try and compete with, particularly when coupled with all the other advantages a number one driver has in a team.

On occasions I felt some people were reluctant to contradict Michael as they seemed scared of upsetting him and of him leaving the team. I have to say that taking life by the balls is not a great strength of all Europeans. When balls were given out in Ireland and England they seem to have run out further south in Europe. But ultimately such an approach may not be good for anyone, least of all Michael himself. There can be a danger of losing perspective on life. It's easy for any of us to become big-headed when you're worshipped! Ask Sonia, she tries her hardest to keep me in line.

As we set off for Brazil in April 1999 there was little I could do about the situation. I was happy to be leading the Championship, although I was under no illusion that I'd have to move over for Michael if he was behind me. But that wasn't new, I'd lived with that for four years. The main issue as we went to Brazil was whether or not we'd caught up with the McLarens.

Brazil is in many respects a great place. They share my view on life in knowing how to enjoy themselves and have a good party. Bearing in mind a lot of Brazilians have very little to be joyful about, it's quite an inspirational country. On this trip I paid a visit to a Samba school in Sao Paolo and picked up a few tips, so I'll be ready for the Carnival in Rio. I'd like to go next year if it fits in with my motor racing commitments. The most depressing thing about Brazil is the poverty. To get to the track you have to drive past rows and rows of the 'Favelas', the slums where people live in shacks, or under flimsy canopies. It brings it home to you just how lucky we are, and that our problems are nothing when compared to those people's problems. One of the main motivational factors in my life has been to make myself financially secure. I'd hate to go back to being poor and not having enough money to enjoy myself and have my toys.

Obviously, my victory in Melbourne hadn't changed anything. I was the Ferrari number two, in spite of press speculation to the contrary. At this point Michael was still calm and confident, declaring that his Championship would start in Brazil, and that his problems regarding his starts had been resolved, and we were all working on improvements to the car. He went on to say that although he was still number one, if during the course of the season I was in a position to fight for the Championship it would be normal for him to help me.

I think what Australia did was make the team realise that if Michael was out of the race, I could be in a position to take over. Maybe that unsettled them a bit, although Jean Todt did consider the possibility when he said in a press conference in Brazil 'What would happen if Eddie wins another race? We'll wait for this to happen and then you'll see how I'll react.' I guess at that point the possibility of Michael being out through injury was so small that no one thought my being in contention for the championship might be an issue that would have to addressed in the months ahead.

It had always been my intention to go eventually to another team as the number one, to join an outfit where I'd have the whole team working for me. For a driver, it's very important to be the centre of attention. In fact, Ferrari is the only team where there is a clear number one status, which of course makes it impossible for the co-driver to be anything other than number two.

With the press conference out of the way we did some testing before the race and in my opinion had the wrong set up. We qualified better than I thought we would on the Saturday, but we were still a bit down about the distance between us and the McLarens. Michael qualified fourth, still a second off Pole man Hakkinen, and I qualified in sixth a second and three tenths off the pace. It wasn't a good situation by any stretch of the imagination. The only comforting thing was that we had teams in front of us who hadn't proved their reliability, whereas our cars might be slow but they had a good chance of finishing the race. As we saw in Australia sometimes the tortoise can beat the hare, and in motor racing it doesn't matter how fast you are, if you don't finish the race, the result is always the same nil points.

In fact, the McLarens proved to be a little more reliable, at least in regard to Mika Hakkinen's car. Coulthard went out with a gearbox problem but Hakkinen took the winner's spot. Personally, I had a terrible race. The car felt strange. The steering seemed extremely heavy and the car was bottoming very badly at the front. I made a good start, but I had to be pretty careful with Michael in front of me. Needless to say, I wouldn't have got any brownie points if I'd taken him off.

At the first pit stop, I changed the angle of the front wing, but it didn't make much difference. Frustratingly, I was then forced to make an unscheduled stop to refill the air supply for the engine's pneumatic valves. After that the situation improved but both Frentzen and Ralf Schumacher had taken advantage of my situation and were in front. I have no doubt that without this problem I would have finished on the podium.

The main lesson from Brazil was that we needed to make aerodynamic improvements for the next race, and we returned to Europe to embark on an extensive test programme before our first European race at Imola, which is one of our home circuits. The good news was that my fifth place in Brazil meant I retained my lead in the World Championship, and so I went to Europe as leader, and that meant a lot to me. The only downside about leading the World Championship was that I remained the focus of press and public attention, and I have always hated people staring at me. I really love being the leader in the team, but I can't bear being the centre of attention outside of Ferrari.

I have never got used to being famous. I really don't like the way some people just gawp at me. When you think about it, you have to admit that standing and staring at people is a bit of a weird thing to do. Once, I was getting out of my car and a guy just came up to me and stood there staring saying 'Irvine, Irvine,' as though I'd just landed from Mars.

I used to be able to go to the Irish Pub in Bologna and sit in the corner and have a few pints, but when I went in there shortly after becoming a Ferrari driver, within five minutes the pub was full of people staring at me. So I had no choice but to leave. In fact the situation is worse in Italy than at home. The Italians seem to have a different mentality when it comes to leaving people alone. If a restaurant is empty, then they will come and sit at the next table. It's the same situation with the boat when I'm down there. I can wake up on a Sunday anchored off Portofino or along the Riviera, go out on deck and it's like Sainsbury's car park. The whole world and their aunt is moored by my boat. The Latins just seem to like cuddling up together. Me? I like my space and my freedom.

Some people get obsessed with this fame thing, particularly in Italy. Over there you can appear on a game show and next thing you know you're in the papers and famous. But at the end of the day it's such a superficial thing, all about looks and clothes. It's not quite the same in Northern

Ireland as we don't really go down the pub on a Sunday in our designer clothes and gold jewellery – if we did we'd seriously get the piss taken out of us – so it's a bit easier to be famous in Northern Ireland and be left alone.

That's one of the reasons why I loved racing in Japan. I was earning money, enjoying my racing, and I was left alone to enjoy life. If I went out to a nightclub, chatted up the girls, got drunk and partied till dawn, it didn't make headlines in the papers like it would in Europe. Having said all that, there is, of course, an upside to fame. I hate queuing and wasting time, and now I can just turn up and get a table in a restaurant. I get into nightclubs for free, and people buy me drinks.

At home in Dalkey the guy before me had chopped down some trees to get a look at the sea. It had caused all sorts of trouble between him and the neighbours, and I had to agree with them. I'd definitely rather be surrounded by trees and have my privacy. After all, I could always walk down to the bottom of the garden and look at the sea. I wanted a forest in my garden, not neat little suburban flower beds which would win me a 'Pretty Garden of the Year Award'. One day the landscape gardener arrived with a load of little shrubs to plant. I said to him 'I don't want little shrubs, I want big trees and bushes.' Particularly when I'm at home, I want to hide away, not be exposed. Anyway the tree-planting has had to take a back seat as I'm rebuilding the house, which was much too small. The new house will have a pool and a 'boys' room with bar, cinema, snooker. It will be a great place to relax in with my friends.

I've got good friends. I've sorted out the true mates from

the hangers on. When I first went to Italy people would invite me to their birthday party or whatever just because of who I am, but I soon worked that out, and I hang out with my true mates and my family, who have always been my biggest supporters. Right now they were all on a high as I arrived back in Europe having won my first race and still leading the World Championship. It didn't change my life, but I felt good. The year was already beginning to have a more positive ring about it. I felt that I was ready for Imola.

CHAPTER 2

The Family

I was born on 10 November, 1965 in Newtownards, Northern Ireland. Being brought up in Northern Ireland has its own advantages and disadvantages – the people are down to earth and open, lacking in the bullshit of the so-called sophisticated races in southern Europe, but the Troubles are also never far away.

I'm not a political animal at all, I never have been and never will be. To put it bluntly, I think all politicians are compromised because they need to win over voters to get elected. However, I was certainly aware of the Troubles when I was growing up. For one thing, you really didn't want to go into certain areas of the city. I have a vivid memory of an occasion when Dad had to drop one of our relatives back to the Falls Road area in Belfast. I was terrified he wouldn't come back. I also remember going into the shops and routinely getting searched. With nothing else to go on, I thought all that carry on was a way of life for everyone. But then I went to England, walked into a shop and waited to be searched, and nothing happened. It was only then that I realised that the way we'd been living in Northern Ireland hadn't been normal at all.

For my part, for what it's worth, I think that we should send Nelson Mandela to Northern Ireland. This is a man who spent practically his whole life in prison but when at last he comes out he doesn't seek revenge. That is incredible, and just the sort of example that is needed in Northern Ireland. Without someone like him who can teach forgiveness, peace will be a long time in coming. At the moment it seems that no one is willing to put the past behind them and move on. One set of people want one thing, and another set want another, neither will compromise so end of story. As far as I'm concerned, if either side really wanted peace then they would give up their arms. If they're not prepared to do without their weapons it must mean that they have no real intention of being peaceful, so if that is the case why do we want to negotiate with them? We might as well forget about it. The only glimmer of hope is in the new generation coming of age now, who are turning to their elders and asking 'Why are we fighting? What is the point of it all?'

There are many worse places to grow up. We've always been very close as a family, and I guess my family know me better than anybody else. At 35 Sonia is eighteen months older than me.

SONIA IRVINE

We had a great childhood. We lived mainly out in the countryside. Most of the time it was just Edmund and I making our own amusements as we didn't have a lot of money. We used to invent our own games building fortresses and secret tunnels in the local haystacks. We'd play by our own rules and if any other children did come to play with us, we'd invariably fall out with them. There wasn't much negotiation in the Irvine household between us kids and outsiders – you did what we said or we didn't play with you!

I used to look after him when we were small and I had to be very protective as we were very small height-wise and the kids tended to pick on Edmund. I am definitely the organiser of the two of us. Edmund was always quite disorganised, it didn't just happen when he reached Formula One. Some people say they go into his hotel room and it looks as if a bomb's hit it, but he's always been like that. I remember once when a friend was looking after our house in Ireland and went into Edmund's room and, because it was such a mess, he actually thought we'd been burgled. He even called up my dad and said 'I think you've been burgled,' but when the friend explained that he'd been into Edmund's room, Dad just said 'No, no, no, Edmund's room's always like that.'

We used to swim quite seriously and I'd always be the organiser as he'd be missing his goggles and things like that, so I suppose I've always looked after him. We'd get up and train before we went to school, and had training sessions after school and at the weekends as well. There is a lot of dedication required to compete seriously in a sport, and swimming took up a lot of our childhood. We must have started aged about ten and carried on until we were sixteen or seventeen. I carried on longer than Edmund did, but I hated getting up in the morning.

My dad had a garage business and sometimes when he'd done a deal, he'd have a load of polystyrene left over, so we'd go out to the nearby river to make a raft. No matter how many times we'd fall in and have to change our clothes, Mum never stopped us, she just smiled and kept loading the washing machine. We've been lucky in having the parents we have. Both of them have always given us a lot of freedom and support. Mum was great and was very innovative in keeping us amused. She would make up competitions for us to play, and she would never say

'You can't do that,' or 'It means more work for me.'
She just let us get on with it, and cleared up uncom-
plainingly afterwards.

My dad used to race single-seater cars and really
enjoyed it, so we got the motor racing bug fairly early
on. Dad would buy an old motor home each year for
us to go on our annual holidays to the British Grand
Prix. He'd check the mechanics and Mum and I would
make curtains and covers. We'd take off in the motor
home and go and visit our cousins in Durham on the
way. We'd park outside the ice rink and Edmund and I
would go in every day to the ice rink and just go
round and round. Even then Edmund was into speed,
he'd see how fast he could go and how far he could
push himself.

In the afternoon we'd go and visit our cousins.
From there we'd go down to Brands Hatch or
Silverstone. Once we got there Mum and Dad would
just say 'Right, see you in there, then,' as they didn't
have the money to pay for us all, and we could slip
under fences whereas they really couldn't. It was just
expected that we would get in by hook or crook. In
fact we always found a way to get in. We'd attach ourselves to other adults, or we'd watch the people on the
admission gates, and whenever their backs were
turned we'd scoot in. One year, when my brother was
nine or ten and I was eleven, Edmund dug a hole and
then scrambled under the fence. I have to admit that I
didn't have the bottle to do that, so I found another
way in. We always made arrangements about meeting
up, but we were also happy to do our own thing. One

year, I think it was 1976, the year James Hunt won the Champion-ship, Edmund managed to get into the pits. That was a bit of a coup.

We're very independent now as adults, both of us are confident and able to work things out for ourselves. We're not scared of being left alone and not being able to cope. I think that maybe that sense of independence was instilled in us as kids. We weren't frightened of not meeting up with our parents once inside the circuit or of losing each other.

His hero at that time was John Watson, and it was great when he won the British Grand Prix in 1981. We would always support John, and it's great that John now supports Edmund. When Edmund won in Australia, John was there and it all got very emotional. He went up to congratulate Eddie, and then turned to me and we both burst into tears.

As a kid Edmund always had a mind of his own. As my mum will say you couldn't really punish Edmund, nothing would ever bother him. If she said 'Go to bed, you're not having your dinner,' he'd just go to bed whistling away, so you never got the feeling that you'd got one over on him. If Mum said 'Go to your room now', he'd just go to his room, put his music on full blast and that would be it, we wouldn't see him for the rest of the day.

It is strange now that he is a Formula One driver and famous. I sometimes have to pinch myself and ask 'Is this all really happening?' When he got his plane, I thought 'My kid brother has his own plane!' It just seemed so unbelievable compared to the days when we all piled into the rickety old motor home and set off for England. So many things have happened that sometimes you need to do a quick reality check and remind yourself that not many people live like this. Not everyone has their own plane and their own boat, and several houses and a collection of expensive classic cars, and jets round the world going to grands prix.

I can relate that to myself as well. We didn't have rich parents but we had a rich childhood. Now I find myself mixing with people in the world of Formula One who have been brought up with a huge amount of material wealth, and have never known what it is like to scrimp and save, to worry about the last penny, to wonder if you can afford that new pair of jeans. But I look at them and think how lucky I am to have had the upbringing I had.

I have to keep my feet on the ground as well. I know that jetting round the world, being part of the Ferrari Formula One team, wearing the uniform, having access to the pits, going to the parties, sharing my life with the team, travelling with the team, isn't what most normal people do. But at the same time I'm not there to enjoy myself but to work, and race weekend is hard work. I'm in charge of Edmund's dietary and physio requirements, and also his business life. When I'm not preparing drinks or food, or taking him to see the sponsors, then I'm on the computer working and planning the next few days or months. It's a seven-days-a-week job, but I'm glad to have had the experience I've had working with Edmund. I've gathered a lot of expertise in how sporting events work and in the world of PR that will stand me in good stead when or if I want to do my own thing.

Before I worked with Eddie I had my own sports physio practice in Kent. Right at the end of 1995 he phoned me to say he'd got the drive at Ferrari and would I like to go and work for him. We agreed money and off I went. I suppose that also changed things as far as our relationship is concerned. He's my brother but also at the end of the day he's my boss, and that does have an effect. You develop a working relationship and that sometimes takes over. A lot of people will just agree with him for the sake of it, but if I don't agree with him then I'll say, 'Well, I'm sorry, but that's not right.' He may not like it sometimes, but at the end of the day he's got to have someone who will keep a little bit of reality in the situation.

I suppose our brother-sister relationship has suffered a bit as we've become more boss and employee, although when Mum and Dad are around we then become like a family again. Occasionally, we manage to get on his boat together as a family and then it is different. It is Edmund's boat, but it becomes more like the family times we used to have, and I value those moments. As he's become more famous it has become more difficult to enjoy even a few quiet moments as a family without someone coming up and interrupting us to ask for his autograph. Edmund hates the kind of attention that comes with fame, he really hates people staring at him. I think that has been the downside to his success, that we've lost some of our family times, not just because of intrusions, but because life is always so rushed now that there is very little time for us to get around the table and eat or talk together.

His is a high-stress career and I try to make sure things run smoothly for everyone's sakes. Edmund hates incompetence and people not doing their job properly makes him blow his top. At one particular grand prix we had to do a photo shoot. There were a lot of press there wanting to talk to him and people everywhere wanting his autograph. It was mayhem. I just knew by the look on his face that he'd had enough. So I went to the press officer and said 'I wouldn't do this next interview if I were you, I really think he's done everything he can.' But they didn't listen and, in a way that was totally out of character, Eddie just turned round and said, 'I'm not doing this,' and walked off. However, things have changed now, both because people listen to what I say and everything goes through me, and also because there's no denying Edmund has changed now. He's more focused and more concentrated than he used to be, so we're really careful about what we put in each race weekend.

My job has expanded a lot since I joined him in 1996. He wanted me to take over more and more aspects of his life, so that now I do a lot of the business side as well, which I enjoy. It's hard work but more stimulating and I have my own projects that I am responsible for. Knowing him as well as I do it is easier to know what he will and won't do, so I can liaise effectively with the sponsors and say 'Yes he'll do this as he's in Rome and can fit it into the schedule,' or 'No we'll have to do that some other time.' The main thing is to try and take advantage when he's in a particular area, and do several appearances so that he isn't always flitting all over the place doing bits and pieces. One thing's for sure, he'd be lost without his plane. He'd be forever in airports and there's no way he would be able to meet all his current commitments. He definitely needs it, it's not just for show.

I really hate rushing which is why I spend a lot of time trying to prepare and make things work smoothly and well. At the end of the day it's less hassle. I think it must be part of the motor racing mentality but Edmund's temperament is that it's always a rush to do things.

It's not that often that Edmund and I fall out, but it does happen. We had words in Montreal this year when I dealt with something in a way I felt was right, but Edmund didn't agree and we ended up shouting and screaming at each other. But when it's over and done with, we're not the sort of people to hold grievances.

Edmund will be driving for Jaguar next year, and that is the end of one era and the beginning of a new one. The four years with Ferrari have been fantastic, but I think I'm probably at the point in my life when I need to sit back and think about the future. I don't want to continue this madcap lifestyle and end up alone at fifty. I'd like to settle down, but I'm sure not going to do it while I just move around between air-ports, countries and grand prix circuits. People are always saying to me, 'Wow, you must meet some incredible men, and always have a choice of whoever you want.' I wish it was like that! I work in a man's world, but I don't think forming relationships within your working environment is a good idea. I don't know if relationships are just more complicated for me but my lifestyle certainly doesn't help, so I know I need to stand back, take a look at things and make some decisions. At present I travel a lot and it is impossible to form a relationship with anyone. I have some very good friends all over the world. They and my family are the most important things to me right now. I have had several different offers for next year, but I haven't yet decided what to do. Eddie would manage without me, he's very adaptable. No one's indispensable and sometimes I think change is good for everyone.

People ask me if I've seen a change in him since he became famous, but I suppose I've seen more of a change in the people around him. I've noticed that when people are with Edmund they do everything in their power to keep his attention, and often I just sit back and watch it all happen. Girls will do all sorts of things to catch his eye – they'll wear the lowest cut dresses, or they'll walk along sticking their boobs or their arses out just to get a bit of attention. But having said that, guys are the same, they'll agree with him whether he's right or wrong. If they want to go to a certain place but Edmund doesn't, they always tag along to where he wants to go. They just want to be in his company and they want to be his friend, although having said that he is good fun, he's very laid back and relaxed and you always have a good time when you go out with him.

Nevertheless I have to say that some of the people who tag along with him have surprised me because I thought they wouldn't be impressed with fame, but would have the confidence to just be themselves. Being proved wrong about people in this way is depressing. Just because someone's famous doesn't mean they're better than anyone else. Fame is not a guarantee of a good character, in fact it can be the opposite, although in that respect I would say that Edmund has still got his feet quite firmly on the ground. He hasn't taken flight yet, and if he does I'm sure we'll all bring him back down to earth. I think being Irish helps as we are not a nation that takes bull-shit very easily.

To be honest, I think he knows who his friends are and who the hangers on are, but at the end of the day he enjoys people's company. He is a sociable person. Although he likes his own space, he doesn't really like being on his own a lot. As most of his friends work, there are often only a limited number of people avail-able to play with him when he has time off. I think he keeps his eyes open and is aware of what's going on but sometimes it suits him to have these people around.

The only thing I have noticed about him is that sometimes he doesn't realise what it's like to live in the real world, how hard it is for ordinary people to live, pay all the bills and keep their heads above water. It costs an awful lot of money to just live today. Our parents do a lot of travelling but they haven't got any income as such, and there are certain things they can do and certain things they can't do. I think that sometimes Edmund is rushing about in his own world and doesn't stop to think of that.

At the moment he is very focused on himself. I suppose most racing drivers are like that because it's part of their job – they can't exactly be Mr Nice Guy and spend all their time thinking about everyone else. Also as soon as they get a reputation for being nice they are hammered in the press. David Coulthard got a reputation for being easy and soft, the sort of reputation a racing driver can't really afford to get. The whole set up is still very macho. The concept of the New Man hasn't quite hit the Formula One circuit yet. Sensitivity is very much perceived as a weakness and they'll do anything to avoid showing any emotion, even if they feel it inside. My opinion is that he has a soft inner part, but to survive in the world of Formula One you have to be very selfish. He was a shy child, and not a girl's lad at all, quite the reverse. If people came to the house, he'd disappear and go to his room and read the *Guinness Book of Records*, and motoring magazines. He always preferred reading to socialising and mixing with people. He's confident now but, underneath it all, there's still the shy little boy. He just covers it up with a confident and fun-loving persona.

Sometimes I do wish he would think a bit more, like when he won in Austria. In the main victory photograph it wasn't actually his own team that were pictured around him, it was Michael's team, and that's because Michael's team are more used to winning and

Edmund's team are less used to pushing in whenever
the official photograph is being taken. For them it's
great to get in the papers as they don't earn a lot of
money and that is the way they can get a bit of glory.
So I organised another photograph with just Edmund
and the trophy and he signed a copy, for each of the
team. I guess that I consider that an important part of
my job, trying to make people happy if I can. That
doesn't make me Mother Teresa, but I think it is vital
that people are made to feel important when they have
made a contribution to success.

Edmund is pretty happy-go-lucky most of the time.
A lot of the time at the race track he can be deep in
thought, but then sometimes he can get a bit aggressive if the race transportations don't go according to
plan or he doesn't get away from the circuit as quickly
as he'd like. I'm sure, though, that this comes from an
adrenalin high. He doesn't really show much emotion.
I remember he cried at our grandmother's funeral in
February, but I've never seen him cry in the way I cry,
or I've seen my dad or mum cry.

He has a pretty wild reputation with women, but
basically he's very upfront with them. Before he gets
involved, he'll say 'This is what I'm like, this is what I
want, and either you like it or you don't like it.' So at
the end of the day it's their decision what they want to
do. If they still want to get involved with him then
they can't complain about the way he is. I think some
of them think they can change him, but the truth is
you can't, he's very wary about getting emotionally
involved. If he says to a girl I don't want involvement,

it means just that, and it's a waste of their energy to try and change his mind.

I have to admit that sometimes I think 'Jesus, what do they see in it all, why are they doing what they're doing?' It just amazes me. Sometimes he'll just sleep with them for one night. I can remember one of his chat-up lines that I once heard him say was 'Right, we're leaving.' And he hadn't even been talking to this girl! He just walked right up to her in a nightclub and said 'Right, we're leaving' and off she went with him, not something I would do. But who am I to judge? Edmund takes the view that women are intelligent and able to make up their own minds, they know what they want, so they get what they want, and everyone's happy. I don't see a lot of his actual girlfriends, because he usually spends time with them on the boat or in Milan and I'm very rarely there. I don't really have that much to do with them. On the whole, the ones he has as girlfriends are really nice ladies.

What he'd say is that there are two types of women: women who are good looking who you would go out with, and then there are the women who are not so good looking, but who are really good fun and with them you have a good laugh. I think in his actual girlfriends he needs both of those characteristics. I can't see him settling down yet, but when he does I think it will be with a girl who combines good looks, intelligence and a strong personality. He needs someone who will stand up to him, who has her own mind.

As for me, I'd never get involved with a racing driver, it's just not my scene, and probably not theirs either. Some of them are good friends. I can go out with David or Michael Schumacher after a race and have a really good time, we both like to dance and let our hair down so we hit the dance floor and get it out of our systems. I can go out as good friends, but then I go to bed on my own. It's a lot less complicated, plus many of the racing drivers are quite unreliable. They don't stick to one woman, and I don't share!

Surprisingly enough, in spite of the fact that Michael is German and therefore you'd think that all of Germany supports him, seventy per cent of Eddie's fan mail comes from Germany. We have an official fan club in England, and we always have a dinner on the Thursday before Silverstone, where Eddie looks in for half an hour. There are some people who write to him regularly. They send him things and write nice letters. My mum keeps the things that are sent in for him in a special box. We are always aware that for some people it is really important for them to have contact with their hero, and they spend a lot of time thinking of little things to send him, especially as good luck charms for the Championship. A lot of people send in photographs and posters to be signed and I organise for him to sign them and then we send them back. It's part of the PR exercise – if people spend time writing to him, then we should make sure that they receive a reply. We also respond to various charitable requests, and help out where we can.

Sometimes when I'm working away in my office in Maranello, near the Ferrari factory, or on the hoof somewhere around the world, or at a grand prix circuit, I'll sit back and think 'Jesus, Eddie could be World Champion.' He really has a fighting chance now. I just take one day at a time, but it seems incredible that he's gone from struggling to get his first break, to actually being in with a chance of winning the big prize. I've total belief that he can do it, and I think the whole of Italy wants him to do it as well. You wouldn't believe the number of people in the pit lane who have come up to us and said 'We know you're from a different team, but we'd love Eddie to win the Championship.'

It seems that since he actually took over from Michael he has become even more focused and determined, with stronger belief in himself and faith that he can do it. I honestly think that if Eddie won the World Championship, he'd be the most popular World Champion for a long time. If the guy who parties can win the top prize, it's good for the sport, good for the commercial interests, and great for Ferrari. Even if he does leave, they'd still have made a World Champion, something they've waited 20 years to do.

Amongst many other things, Sonia has tried to educate me about diet. She tries to teach me things and leaves articles lying around on the subject, but I have to admit that I've always liked my fry-ups and Fray Bentos pies, and that hasn't changed. When I lived with Pete we had a contact at Fray Bentos and a spare room full of things. Pete ate all the puddings and I ate all the pies. It was perfect. Mum will still cook me steaks, sausages, pies and mince and that's the kind of food I was brought up on. I'm not sure about all this obsession with healthy eating. To be honest, it's not as though we're trying to run 1500 metres. Michael's supposed to be a real fitness freak but I've seen what he eats and it isn't good. I think it says it all that the best driver around eats so much junk. You name it, he'll eat it, cakes, ice cream, chocolate, the lot, and it doesn't slow him down.

However, I think the key point that Sonia got me to take on board was ensure I have enough fluid on race day. If you become dehydrated, it can affect your performance. It can damage your concentration and co-ordination, which, needless to say, is not good for a racing driver. During one race I did feel this had actually happened to me so now I take my fluid bottle on board with me, and that prevents me from becoming dehydrated. Sonia makes me up a special carbohydrate concentrated drink, and I have that now throughout the race weekend.

I did learn a lesson when we were in Brazil and I fancied a burger. Sonia warned me it wasn't the best thing to be eating, but I thought I'd be fine. The next day I was down with a slight dose of food poisoning. Fortunately, from Brazil we went to Argentina so I had a few days to recover, but I've learnt that you have to be very careful when you go to foreign countries. Sonia always washes the fruit and vegetables in bottled water, and I take more care about what I eat. Basically it's not worth taking the risk. Some of the drivers have been really unwell in South America after eating or drinking something that wasn't in the best state of cleanliness.

I try to avoid eating solids before going out driving, as it just feels heavy in my stomach and is hard to digest when you're in the car. I have muesli or any carbohydrate cereal for breakfast. Then, after breakfast, toast and jam, which keeps my carbohydrate level up. I don't have a problem with protein, as I love eating chicken. I'm not so keen on fish, but I like Parma ham and mozzarella cheese, and, of course, I get protein from the milk on the cereal. But the most important thing for me to eat is carbohydrate as that gives me the energy I need. After qualifying and after the race Sonia will normally have different things prepared for me, like chicken pasta, or a potato-based vegetable soup. Later on, I'll usually have something like shepherd's pie, mashed potato and chicken, but with plenty of vegetables. When I'm training and racing I need about 3000 calories a day. That might seem a lot but it's not when you're living life at the pace we do. I don't have a weight problem, weight problems occur when you get older usually, eat more and do less exercise!

I am very lazy when it comes to going to the gym. Basically I get bored. I know all the theory of exercise, how to work the upper limbs, lower limbs, trunk and neck, but I just go about it in a more interesting way. I'll go on the boat and go out on the stand-up jet ski. People say that's not the way to train, but my back muscles and all my upper body muscles have been built up incredibly well on the jet ski, so maybe they don't know what they're talking about. I windsurf and go out on my bike but I don't do a lot of running because it is a jarring, high-impact sport which can affect my back. You don't have to do mindless stomping on the treadmill to get fit, and the more people that know this, the better. I think it's about time we all learnt that exercise can be exciting and fun.

My back is a crucial area as I have had a real problem

with finding a comfortable driving seat. I spent the first year or two driving around in agony, until at some point my back muscles would just go numb and then it would get a bit easier. Basically, the car was made for Michael and to fit in with FIA regulations; I was just being crammed into the seat. As my spine is quite long there simply wasn't enough room. For about four months we tried to sort out the problem with the help of Lear, but didn't really get anywhere. They were great, though, and took us down the road they thought was right, but drivers come in all shapes and sizes, and I just don't fit into the standard seat.

Before Japan we started from scratch again. I sat in the car with only the basic cage in place. We had already tried using soft foam of varying thickness to absorb my body-weight as I went round corners, but it hadn't achieved anything. So this time we changed it and used another form of absorption. At last this gave me more support with the result that I could relax my muscles more. We went to Japan and I drove without a problem.

At the start of this year it was a lot easier to get the seat right, as we knew what we had to do. We scanned the old foam seat and made a carbon seat from it, which was meant to be exactly the same as last year's. But when we put it in the car, hey presto, it didn't fit! The Italians had lengthened this a little bit, widened that, and shortened the other, so it simply wasn't the same space. To them it didn't seem to matter, but their changes had made my seat useless. So it was back to the beginning and now I have the basic seating position with a little bit of extension and padding to stop me moving around so much.

If you're not comfortable you can't concentrate, and if you lose hundredths of a second someone overtakes you. It's paying attention to all the details that's important, something Michael is particularly good at. He makes sure his seat is right and he'll also ensure his microphone is directly in front of his mouth so that radio communication between the team is good.

In contrast my communication hadn't been so good, as the material used in my balaclava wasn't as elastic as Michael's, so the microphone was moving around distorting transmission. Now, by going down a size in the balaclava, the microphone is held in a good position and radio communication is much better. It's about improving the whole package and Sonia and Luca work well in sorting the details in terms of seat position, radio communication and airflow around the helmet.

Sonia is a trained physio and that's why I took her on in 1996. She had taken a break out of physio and was backpacking round the world. We met up with our parents in Adelaide, and I asked her to come and work for me. I think it was quite hard at first for her at Ferrari. Not because she was dealing with men – seventy per cent of her practice had consisted of male clients – it was more the language problem and also maybe the fact she was my sister. At first they didn't quite know how to treat her. But she gradually got settled in, starting to do physio for some of the rest of the team if they needed it. She sorted out someone's shoulder problem and after that they realised that she really was a qualified physio, and not just my sister.

By the end of the first year her job was expanding and she was organising everything for me over the race weekend, such as PR events and getting me in and out of the circuit. As she always knew where I was it seemed sensible for her to take over my diary as well to make sure I did the press interviews and sponsors appearances as per schedule. This part of her job has got busier and busier. The requests for press interviews have increased considerably since Silverstone, and I've had to try to cut down on how many I do over the race weekend. There are so many other meetings and pressures that to stay focussed I need to have minimum interruptions. But it isn't always easy. Even if I'm in the middle of a test, someone wants an interview. If you're not careful it can get out of control and Michael is absolutely right in just refusing to do anything. But people know I'm a different personality and so they keep on trying. Non-stop.

CHAPTER 3

Imola

Arriving at Imola things felt pretty good. As it was Italy, though, naturally the gossips were out in full force. There was the usual speculation about Michael wanting a new team mate, and about Ferrari talking to other drivers for next year. Well, nothing new there then. Ferrari always talk to everyone, and as I've said before Michael is very important to Ferrari. I'd felt for a time that I was getting a little too close to him in terms of speed and overall performance.

I don't have any personal problems with Michael, we meet on the track and get down to business. Away from the track we don't meet. It's not a problem being a different nationality, I have German friends, but we just have completely different mentalities. As a driver, you couldn't pay me to have Michael's life. We like totally different things. I first met him in 1989 or 1990, and I remember thinking 'Wow that guy is a bit good.' He won the race so I wasn't far wrong. Now we're colleagues, but I don't see him from one race to the next. In fact there are only two or three people in the Ferrari outfit I go out with, and I think Michael only goes out with Jean Todt. But that's motor racing, we do tend to keep ourselves to ourselves. It's not what you'd call a matey sport.

But the mood in the team now was good. We'd made improvements to the car and so we felt we should be up to speed. We'd put in some hard work testing in Jerez in Spain, concentrating on a new front wing. This was a combination of the V shape we introduced last year and the end plates used in the French Grand Prix, and it was intended to give us greater speed and flexibility. Michael tested it on the Thursday before the race and then he used it again in Friday practice. We both had it for Saturday's qualifying which went better than the last two races. I thought the new wing had made a slight improvement to the car; it wasn't incredible, but in a sport where thousands of a second count, it could make the difference between victory and coming second.

I qualified fourth just over seven tenths of a second off Pole man Mika Hakkinen, so although I was happy with my position, I was a lot less happy with my time. I lost half my quick laps because of yellow flags and in those conditions it is difficult to improve. Although the two McLarens were on the front row, we felt that we'd made some progress in catching up, and overall I felt we were in a better position now than at this time last season. Michael was only two tenths of a second off Hakkinen. Annoyingly, though, they decided to cancel the race morning drivers' briefing. The new rules this year force drivers to attend a briefing on the Friday morning, before we first go on the track. Whereas previously there was a compulsory meeting on the Sunday, it is now down to the race director. I'm not crazy about this as most of the drivers, me included, can't remember what we talked about four hours before, let alone two days before.

I was second in Sunday's warm up session so I felt good about the race. Soon after the start, though, I started having trouble with the car's handling as it was moving around a lot on the soft tyre. After that it stabilised and my lap times came down again. In spite of the problem, I'd maintained my fourth position from the start, and stayed like that until Mika Hakkinen made a mistake on lap 16 and went into the pit-straight barriers. It was to be the first of several such moments for Hakkinen, which is great for us guys just behind him. After moving up to third behind Michael and DC I was pretty confident of a podium finish. Then, on lap 47, I felt the engine tighten. About 100 metres later, it blew. For the second consecutive race, I'd missed out on an almost certain top three finish. It was disappointing to say the least.

Once again it was Ross Brawn's ability as a master strategist that won us the race through Michael Schumacher. I think that Ross's strength is his flexibility regarding strategy. A lot of teams will decide, for instance, whether it is a one stop, or two stop race before the start, and stick to it whatever happens. Ross, on the other hand, will say 'Right, we have an option of this and this, so let's see how it's going and then we can decide during the race.' This was vital at Imola. The two stop strategy gave Michael the opportunity to do a fast mid-race sprint. During the 14 lap middle run Michael was probably doing qualifying speeds, so he could stay ahead of DC, and in the end that won him the race.

DC had a bit of a carp about drivers not letting him through. However, at Spa last year I felt he should have let Michael through a lot earlier. I don't think he did it deliberately but it wasn't a great piece of driving, that's for sure. It wasn't a great bit of stewarding either, as I felt DC held Michael up for too long. In my view he should have been pulled into the pits and given a ten second penalty, or given a penalty after the race for holding up the leader. However if I'd been in Michael's position, I might have been a little less hasty to push on past him. Michael was 35 seconds up the road, there was no need for him to be in such a hurry. I have to say I was surprised Michael drove back to the pits as it was quite dangerous with three wheels and the front destroyed. But as we saw, he wasn't exactly in a relaxed frame of mind!

Spa 1998 had its dangerous moments for me as well. I was part of the big pile up after the start of the race. That, I have to admit, was a bit scary. I had no brakes, no steering, nothing was working. I was just sitting there hurtling down the track with wheels hitting me on the head and cars going all over the place. There was nothing I could do except sit there and think 'Shit, where is this taking me?' It was not pleasant. I try not to think about accidents and I try and avoid them. I want to stay alive.

But fear is an irrational business. The things that really scare the shit out of me are earwigs, which used to infest our house in Ireland. I'd rather do 180 mph round Monza than even see an earwig, let alone have one crawling around on me. I don't like snakes, either, but they are about the only two things that scare me, except for weddings, of course, and commitment, but that's another story!

A couple of good friends of mine have lost their lives in motor racing. Roland Ratzenberger and Jeff Krosnoff were two such friends. Jeff in particular was a very close mate, you couldn't find a nicer guy, uncomplicated, fun and down to earth. It was a real loss and I was very shaken by his accident, and sad I couldn't go to the funeral as Ferrari kept me back to do some work. Spa did not bring back good memories and neither was it too good for my mum and dad, who were at the track.

E D M U N D   S E N I O R

I have to admit that my heart seemed to stop after the accident at Spa. I hate watching the start anyway, as it's dangerous and here I could see wheels and wings flying about. I ran down the pit lane as fast as I could to see what had happened. Eddie has a very distinctive helmet and halfway down I could see his helmet coming out of the car as he stood to get out. I knew then that he was alright.

Eddie's closest friend as a driver was Jeff Krosnoff, who raced with Eddie in Japan. They'd done Le Mans together with Toyota, and finished second. We had swapped helmets and Jeff's helmet is in my house in Ireland. Then Jeff left to do Indy car and he was killed in Toronto in 1996. Eddie was at the British Grand Prix when he heard the news from his friend and journalist, Adam Cooper. It was the first time I've seen Eddie lose his temper. Someone asked for his autograph and he just lost his cool, said he wanted to go. He was staying in Oxford, and he watched the race to see what had happened, because I think he needed to know. He took it really badly. He wanted to go to the funeral but Ferrari said they needed him to work, so Kathleen and I went over to Los Angeles. It was nice we could go and meet his parents and his wife, because I'd met Jeff in Japan, and he was a genuine friend.

Jeff was a very special sort of person. He was never jealous of Eddie's success. Whenever Eddie had success in Formula One, Jeff was genuinely pleased for him. He would ring him up and say, 'You used to be mega, now you're a giga!' He was a great guy.

KATHLEEN IRVINE

I usually go for a walk at the start of a race as I don't like it. Suddenly, I saw Sonia running one way and my husband running the other. I knew something was wrong and I just stood there frozen to the spot. Then Sonia sent word that everything was alright.

It's his decision to race. I can't tell him what to do, and in fact I've never been heavy handed with the kids, they had to learn their way. All I did was support them and try to make life as good for them as possible. But I have to admit that it's hard with a son, you always worry about him. When my husband was racing I used to just wonder what he was up to. But with my son it's different; my heart is in my mouth.

There's very little chance of my mum getting caught for speeding. She is slow in the extreme. If ever you see a queue of traffic you can be sure my mum is at the head of it. One year after the British Grand Prix we had a bit of a party, and mum was volunteered to drive. It took us about two hours to get to Oxford and there was no traffic. She must have been doing about 15 mph, and that wasn't even in the camper van but in my Mercedes. It didn't annoy me, I just put my head back and went to sleep.

I, on the other hand, go as fast as I think is safe. I've done 185 mph in Italy. Once I was travelling to Milan from Monaco at about two or three in the morning. I hadn't had a drink and, wanting to get back before everything closed, I did the journey in an hour and a half, which wasn't particularly healthy. I wouldn't like to do that again. We actually went past the police at 160 mph at one stage, but the

Italian police weren't that particularly worried. They normally recognise me and ninety per cent of the time, they just say 'On you go, take it easy.' But I wouldn't recommend those kind of speeds to anyone else (or to myself, come to that!). As a professional driver you're trained to react quickly at very high speed, but if you're not a professional you can make a mistake and very easily end up dead.

I was done once for speeding, and actually that was the safest bit of speeding I've done. I was doing 102 mph on an empty motorway in Cumbria, and the only two cars on the motorway were me and the police car. I lost my licence for two weeks. The British police are a lot less tolerant than the Italians. They do their job by the rule books. I accept that doing 101 mph round the M25 in the rush hour would be foolhardy, but doing 101 mph in Cumbria with no other cars around in a motor that's capable of doing twice that, is not so dangerous in my opinion.

Having said that, I have learnt by my mistakes. I never take chances on the road. I was involved in a crash as a passenger and although it wasn't scary for me, it was for the two other people who weren't so used to having accidents. By the time I got my hand across to the wheel it was better to keep spinning. Next thing we hit the barrier and the girl's head hit the window. In the blink of an eye, my telephone was sitting on the hard shoulder, my wallet on the central reservation, and the rear view mirror was stuck into my mate's hand. Both front seats had collapsed and I found myself between my mate's legs in the back seat. My mate was in shock and the girl was crying, but we were lucky to get away with what we did. I was quite surprised at how hard we hit the barrier, but we were lucky we were going so fast, because we were still spinning in front of the other cars and they got a chance to slow down. It could have been very serious; the car was destroyed. As I'm involved in a dangerous sport, people often ask if I believe in God. I'm divided, I don't pray or go to Church but I think there's something out there. But how do you work out what it is?

What a difference a year makes. Going into the Monaco Grand Prix Michael was leading the Championship and I was second, just four points behind him. It was all so different to 1998 when the McLarens were already charging ahead of us and everyone was saying Hakkinen would be the World Champion.

I like Monaco as the twisty, street circuit tends to favour skill over power. However, it is a hard race for both car and driver. The cars are set up for maximum downforce to cope with the tight corners, unlike the fast circuits like Monza and Hockenheim where downforce is kept to a minimum. Ride height is a little higher to cope with the hilly circuit. A lap of Monaco is tough for the driver due to the nature of the place. We go from speeds of 270 kph on the pit straight to brake into Saint Devote corner, which is a second gear right hander, and this produces about 3.5 G under braking.

Beau Rivage is the incline, which leans slightly to the left, and there we'll reach over 260 kph, before turning left into Massenet, a 125 kph third gear corner. Then comes the Casino, which is taken in second gear at 115 kph. We then reach about 210 kph as the circuit then goes downhill for about 150 metres, before the Mirabeau, a hard second gear right hander, where we go around a large wall that separates the road from houses. We have little time before we reach Loews, the extremely tight 40 kph hairpin. The short blast from Loews to Virage de Portier goes further down hill, and then there are two right handers.

The harbour then comes into view, before we go through the tunnel and reach speeds of up to 300 kph. Then we have to brake hard to take Nouvelle Chicane, a makeshift s-bend, which is taken at 55 kph in second gear. Drivers then accelerate hard, down a small straight, towards Tabac, a left handed third gear kink. We hardly lose any speed before coming into the left handed Piscine, a left right kink, situated next to Monaco's swimming pool. We then weave our way through another right left kink, hitting speeds of 160 before hitting La Rascasse, another slow hairpin, taken at 40 kph in second gear. Following that is a small straight, where you can hit full speed for about half a second, before coming to Anthony Noghes, a tricky right handed 65 kph second gear kink, which is crucial to get right if you want to shave off time from the competition.

This year we were much closer to the McLarens in qualifying in terms of times. I got fourth, but not as fast as I would like. I made a mistake on my penultimate run and then my last one was okay, but not quite good enough. I was losing time in the first section as I had a lot of understeer through Casino Square. I had spent Friday trying to get rid of understeer, because it is the worse complaint here. There's no doubt that the less understeer I had, the quicker I went. One of the main problems at Monaco is overtaking. It's tough on other circuits but it's impossible here. I was hopeful at the beginning of the race as I usually make good starts, but it wasn't so easy from fourth place.

However, the McLarens helped us out on that. Hakkinen made a poor start with a lot of wheel spin and Michael went past him, DC made an equally poor start and I got up to third, which is where it looked like I might finish. I was lucky to get away with touching the barriers at the Nouvelle Chicane. Then I overtook Hakkinen on the pit stops and once in second place kept it all the way to the finish line. So with Michael taking the race it was one-two for Ferrari, a first for the team at Monaco. Jean Todt and the rest of the team were ecstatic.

I often go to Monaco with the boat as it's a fun place to hang out, but very expensive, which is why I don't understand why we have to have the drivers' trade union, the GPDA (Grand Prix Drivers' Association) offices there. I'm a part of the GPDA but I'm having second thoughts now for a couple of reasons. It gives an opinion, but I don't think you need the GPDA to give an opinion. The most dangerous corners in Formula One are still there, so what has it achieved? We can't even agree on insurance. If we all got together and used the same insurance company we'd get a big discount, but we can't even agree on that. I don't think it's achieved very much. In my view the only reason that changes have been made in Formula One to improve safety is because of the deaths of Roland Ratzenberger and Ayrton Senna.

There was the best party of the year after our one-two at Monaco. My boat, the *Anaconda*, had just come back from being repainted so I had some friends on board. We got the red bull and vodkas in and partied most of the night. A friend of mine had once said to me 'When you have the money, buy a boat,' and I had thought that I needed a boat like I needed a hole in the head. The first time I was on a boat was about 10 years ago, and I didn't particularly enjoy it. It was down in Marbella with a friend of mine, the water was a little bit cold as it was Christmas, and the toilets weren't nice, the showers weren't nice, it was more like camping. Then, just before Monaco 1998, I bought the Anaconda and I've since discovered you couldn't spend your money in a better way. This is a house on the sea. They're expensive and you can lose your shirt on them, but if you're very careful the way you go in and the way you run it, you can make it an acceptable part of your expenses. I had to spend a reasonable amount of money on it as I wanted a boat I could live on. As far as square footage is concerned, this is actually bigger than my house in Dublin. It all began when I started to think about a holiday home and then I hit on a problem – where would I buy it? Dublin is great but the weather is awful. I went to Spain, to Marbella and Puerto Banus and near there and it was horrible, really awful. So I went to the south of France, which I thought was very nice but then I considered that it would get cold there in winter. Finally I came to the conclusion that I'd need about three houses, so I started looking at boats instead. I saw the Anaconda and really liked it, so we started negotiating. Alan Nee, my pilot and a really shrewd businessman, advised me to go in low, and in the end we got it.

There's nothing I miss in not having a house, except

maybe the TV. I don't need a garden, the ocean's my garden and it changes every day. There's every creature comfort on this boat – I've got a proper bathroom, a proper sized bed, and a sauna in my bedroom. Sometimes I think it would be nice to have six bedrooms instead of five, but if I did have six, I'd probably want seven and that would mean four crew and too much more aggro. You see bigger boats in Monaco and St. Tropez, but no one has more fun out of their boat than I do. Some people buy big boats, park in the harbour and then sit and have dinner on the back of the boat, and people stand there watching them eat. I haven't figured out why they do that. I'd want someone to pay me to take my boat into the harbour. You can't just wake up and dive in, you've got to get in your tender and drive out to sea because the water in the harbour is disgusting. You've not got the same freedom there. Being out at sea and being in the harbour is like the difference between having your own country estate and living in a block of flats. In fact I do plan to get hold of a place in Italy with perhaps fifty acres, very hilly with a river running through it, but in the meantime I like life on the ocean, being a kind of jet set gypsy, cruising on the waves. It's the best way for me to get my peace. I can be with who I want and be left alone. If I stay in hotels I've always got people I don't know around me, staring or intruding in some way. On the boat I can be myself, I can relax, take the jet ski out, swim or just hang around on board.

I usually anchor out of the port, especially in Italy where I get bothered a lot. Sometimes I'll go to a restaurant, especially if I'm in Antibes or St. Tropez, but mostly I just stay on board the boat. My usual ports of call are

Villefranche, Portofino, Capri, St. Tropez Ponza, and occasionally Barcelona. I've tried to make the *Anaconda* home with the interior designed as I want it, clean and bright, and I have abstract paintings, including a brilliant blue one by Bea de Silva, hanging on the wall. The Captain is Jonathan Russell, and he looks after her with Rupert Clarke. Jonathan holds a masters certificate and was brought up on a boat but working for me is probably not quite the usual type of job. I tend to make last minute decisions, call him and then he'll cruise to where I want to join the boat, pick me and my friends up and we'll have a few days relaxing. He is also responsible for making sure we don't run out of provisions, and he cooks for us.

I've never really been on the boat on my own. Sometimes my sponsors will use it, or we use it for business meetings, but most of the time it's just a pleasure boat, steaming along the seas with me and my mates partying.

Jonathan Russell

When I met Eddie in 1998, I was working on a racing boat. I looked after the *Anaconda*, which is an 85-foot motor boat, on and off for a month before taking over in the summer of 1998. We're based at Marina Degli Aregai, which is cheap, clean and easy to get to. It's 80 miles from Corsica, 70 miles from Portofino, and 62 miles from St. Tropez, so we have everything in an accessible circle.

A boat of this size would be about £5.5 to 6 million new, but I'm sure Eddie got it for a good price, as he's very astute with his money. It costs about $1,000 a night to dock somewhere like Portofino, but we have a very good deal at Marina Degli Aregai. Running a boat like this takes plenty of organisation in terms of making sure we have adequate fuel, water and provisions. We get through about 20,000 litres of water a week and we've got five fuel tanks on board which take 19,000 litres of fuel. We use about 80 litres an hour when we're sailing, or 150 if we're flat out, 75 to 80 in eco mode. A rough sea will push fuel consumption up. Two large generators power the boat, one to run it and one on stand by. We can run the sauna, washing machine, tumble dryer and dishwasher on one. They consume negligible amounts of fuel which makes them ideal.

Living on a boat isn't an easy option, it's not a case of arriving home and flitting around with a duster, or running a vacuum over the carpet, although that is also part of the job. Salt water is very corrosive and so to keep the boat in tip top condition we have to clean it thoroughly and try and keep wear and tear down to a minimum. The *Anaconda* is a serious boat, it's a Dutch Hakvoort and they are built to last. This one could still be sailing in 80 years, but it will need a re-fit soon. It is ten years old and hasn't been touched in that time, so we need to do some work, but then it will just go on and on.

When Eddie's friends are here we get through about six cases of beer in a week, three cases of Fanta, three cases of Coke, three cases of Sprite, four cases of Red Bull, a case of vodka, and two bottles of gin. On a practical level we'll get through six maxi packs of kitchen rolls a week and four squeezy tubes of Mr

Muscle. Having a working television on board is complicated as it's difficult to keep the satellite dish in place with the movement of the sea. It is very expensive, it can be done but it costs a lot and the reception is never that good. We have a video and films on board. We're going to get a full size screen and then it will be like sitting in a floating cinema.

Working for Eddie is challenging as he usually just rings and says 'Meet you in Portofino in an hour,' and we're in Monaco! It keeps you on your toes, and we've never failed to pick up the boss. Sometimes it can be great fun. Once he and his friend Marcus turned up in Portofino. I walked into the bar where they were waiting for us and they had eight really stunning ladies with them, all different nationalities, all beautiful and all good fun. That's the good thing about Eddie, he lives life to the full. When he has to work he does, but when he relaxes he does that totally as well.

The longest journey we've done is from Gibraltar to the south of France. That was over nine hundred miles and took us four days. The shortest hop is from base to Monaco, which is an hour. The boat is very much his home, but we're also going to make it a business from next year and start chartering it. For Monaco weekend, we can charter it for about $80,000 especially if Eddie does a visit during the weekend. For that we'll have a professional cook onboard.

Last Monaco we had 48 people for lunch and 67 for the party after the race. It's hard work, but I enjoy life, and so does Rupert, who helps me run the boat. He is a friend of Eddie's who has come down to run things for a couple of months. Together we try to sort things out to the best of our ability. Running a boat is a big responsibility, it's not like a house, it can drift off anchor and you have to constantly check and re-check what's happening. We'll often get up three or four times in the night to check whether we're still in the same position, particularly if we have bad weather, when the boat needs a lot more attention.

The most relaxing moments for us are when everyone leaves, otherwise it really is 24 hours a day. Eddie uses the boat a lot more than other owners would. He's probably on the boat about 14 to 16 days a month during the summer. Even in the winter he comes on it, as he'll use the bikes and go up to the hills on them. In effect he uses the *Anaconda* more like a villa, rather than just a boat. We don't have that many parties, probably just after a grand prix, which is quite a good thing. You arrive with a perfect boat and the next morning it's absolutely trashed, and the hard work starts in clearing it up. But having said that it's a good life, I wouldn't change it.

From Monaco it was on to Barcelona and things were looking a lot better than they had in 1998, when the McLarens were sweeping ahead of everyone. Enrico and I had booked a room with a twin bed at the Alfa, which is the hotel nearest the circuit. However, when we arrived at the hotel we were in for a nasty surprise – we were shown to our room, opened the door, and there was only one bed. Now Enrico and I get on well, but not that well! We'd booked a long time ago, but unfortunately we'd been upstaged by an unknowing Michael Schumacher, who had decided not to stay in Barcelona as planned and so had moved into the Hotel Alfa, and all the rooms had got mixed up. Michael didn't know that things had been rearranged in his favour and that Enrico and I had nearly had to share a bed. It wasn't a great start to the weekend.

When I got in the car on Friday it felt good straightaway. However there was a strong wind, so that made it difficult to be sure of the exact situation, and it caused me to lose the rear end of the car and spin during the morning. The wind problem was worse than last year as the tyres now offered less grip, so we have to rely more on aerodynamics. At the end of the session we made some changes to the set up, which improved the car in some parts of the track, and made it worse in others. I was happy to be quickest although that doesn't mean much as you don't know what the other team are doing. Are they practising on full tanks? Half tanks? New tyres? Race set up? But the car was certainly performing better than at last week's test. Everywhere we had been so far in 1999, the car had been really well balanced.

The next day I out-qualified Schumacher to get on the front row of the grid next to Pole man Mika Hakkinen, only just over one tenth of a second behind, which was a great result. The Circuit de Catalunya in Barcelona is tough on tyres due to the abrasive surface, so we always have to watch tyre wear and that influences our pit stop strategy. When the tyres go off it makes the car difficult to drive, so sometimes you have to risk an extra pit stop, and the time lost in that, to protect your position on the track, which would be lost if you had serious tyre wear. The car remained well balanced all weekend, but losing half an hour on Saturday morning might have cost me pole. We could make the car quick in the first section or quick in the final one, but we could not put a whole lap together. In addition to that, on my best lap, I made a mistake in the middle section. I did all my runs early as I felt the track was getting slower. My strategy for the race was to pull away from everyone at the start, get in the lead, and win.

Unfortunately, things didn't quite work out that way. The disadvantage of being in second place was that I was on the dirty side of the track. By that I mean the side where you can pick up debris from the line of the track, and that means it can be more difficult to get grip at the start. This is exactly what happened to me. I got off the line well, but then had too much wheelspin. I was really surprised by the lack of traction. DC was very close and braked earlier than I anticipated, so I had to brake too, and that allowed Jacques to come through. My only actual problem during the race was when the fuel flap came open.

However, it was a pretty dull race, not good for the drivers and not good for the sport. Maybe we have too much testing at Barcelona, and that makes it boring, but whichever way there was a moment during the race when I wished I'd had my stereo in the car to keep me amused. In all, it could have been better in Barcelona, but it could have been worse. One thing's for sure, if you were German, being in Barcelona wasn't much fun just then. I'm not a great football fan, but I do take an interest in Manchester United, who had an incredible season, culminating in that fantastic win over Bayern Munich, when they scored two goals in extra time. The Bayern Munich players thought they had it in the bag, they were beginning to celebrate before the full time whistle, then suddenly it was all over, and they'd lost. That's how it is in sport, you can be cruising to victory, and something will happen, and everything changes.

After a dull race in Spain, Canada was going to be a lot more exciting, with action and a few surprises in store. I was hoping to get some points and regain the lead in the Drivers' Championship, although that seemed pretty unlikely unless Michael decided to give up motor racing and go fishing. At that point there was more possibility of me getting married than of that happening.

CHAPTER 4

Friends

Friends have always played an important part in my life. I hang out with friends, party with friends, work with friends, it's part of the Irvine way of life. Some of the friends are very different, some are similar, but all have a role to play in my life. I like to be surrounded by my own friends and I don't like people around me whom I don't know. With my own little band nobody tries to dominate the conversation or be a pratt. People think famous people are arrogant but it's funny how some people change when a famous person comes near them. They just talk rubbish and expect you to talk rubbish back. Another driver once sent two of his friends to St. Tropez and I said I'd look after them. Never again, they were awful! They wanted to be centre of attention and ruined our night through being arrogant and obnoxious. One of them got thrown out of the nightclub and that reflects badly on me. My little band might misbehave but we don't affect other people. The bottom line is that my life is so busy that I haven't got time for idiots. My free time is very precious and I want to make the most of it. In fact I'd say I'm pretty reclusive now except when I party! Even then I prefer to go to places where they know me and people don't bother me

PETER FOX, PHOTOGRAPHER

I met Eddie in 1989 when he was doing Formula 3000. We just started talking at the track and he mentioned he was looking for somewhere to live in Oxford, because he'd just started driving for Eddie Jordan, also in Formula 3000. I was working for Mark Gallagher at the time, and he'd known Eddie for a while. He also knew Eddie Jordan who arranged for Eddie to stay at Mark's house where I was living as well.

At first I thought he was awkward, quite rude even, then I realised he was like that because he was shy. I find that most people who are shy come across as rude. Once you got to know him and he trusted you, and he knew you weren't there to make money out of him, he was just a normal bloke. He really is a normal bloke who happens to drive a racing car. I think we get on because I enjoy life, I do the things I want to do, I really like to have a good laugh and I like my women, which is always a good way to get on with Eddie.

Even so we are totally different people. I'm not so much into material things and money. I suppose I'm more of a hippie. But although Eddie is a messy sod, he was really laid back to live with as he just does his own thing. We used to just sit around eating Fray Bentos pies and tinned peas and dodgy mashed potatoes. But because we both travelled a lot – I was away photographing F3000 and the grand prix and he was driving – we didn't really have much of a social life at that time. We were just passing ships in the night.

He moved out a year later, went off to Japan and we ocasionally spoke on the phone and kept in contact. Macau was when we spent most time together. I was photographing the Macau Grand Prix in 1989 and he was driving in it. He was going out with Maria so he'd stay at her place, and we used to go to a load of clubs and bars. Maria would tell me where to find the girls and Eddie would point out who I should go for. He wasn't in the market as he was firmly going out with Maria.

He does care about things, but I think he's been very fortunate in the way it's come together for him. I think he likes people who have got their own personality and can stick up for themselves. He's surrounded by a lot of yes men, who want to get something out of him, but he can see through that, he's not stupid. He may not admit it but he's pretty astute about people's characters; he can sum people up pretty quickly and he's usually right. Sometimes, though, I don't know if he appreciates how lucky he is.

He is very switched on about business and making money. He has great respect for money and doesn't throw it away. You might say that he's not one to open his wallet, but he's careful rather than mean. He's very generous to his friends, has us on the boat and things, but he wouldn't chuck money around. He keeps his eye on the business side of things, and nothing gets past him. He's certainly got a great ability to make money. We'd come home from the pub at Christmas or New Year completely slaughtered, and he'd be there with the remote control looking at share prices. He was always on the ball all the time.

All the racing drivers are all given an image by the media, and to some degree they end up living up to that image. He can be a bit wild, but I've never seen him go on a real bender. He's always been ambitious, but quietly so. There was one occasion when he came back from the German Grand Prix having won the F3000 race at Hockenheim and he just walked in through the front door and said 'Ah ha, je suis un fucking mega . . . .' but he doesn't do that very often. I think that first win was a huge boost to his confidence, like the first Formula One win this year.

Mind you, sometimes I don't know how he's got where he has, as he's so disorganised. We always had this pact in the house that whoever was last out of the house would shut the doors and windows, like most people do. When he was away winning that race in Hockenheim, I came back and thought 'Fuck, we've been burgled.' The front door and all the windows were open. I went up to the bathroom and found the toilet unflushed and the bath full of scummy water. Next I went down to the kitchen which I noticed seemed rather warm. That was when I noticed that the oven was on. A Fray Bentos crusted pie had been left there for four days on a low heat. All that remained was this little bit of dried up, flattened crust, it was completely frazzled. I checked out the rest of the house and nothing had been stolen, so I called Eddie. 'Oh yeah, I'm in Germany,' he said. 'Must have forgotten to lock up.' He'd left the house like that and just gone. His mind was away. For a guy who's never done drugs sometimes he's incredibly spaced out.

Another time he really did get me into trouble. For the first time in ages I had to go to the doctor as I had a really bad sore throat. In a short time the doctor's face lengthened. 'Now Mr Fox,' he said, 'I'd like to have a little chat with you. I really think you should be taking more responsibility with your sexual partners.' I was taken aback. It was a sore throat, not a raving dose of the clap. He went on 'There has been at least one instance here of emergency contraception being issued to you.'

'What are you talking about?' I asked. 'I've never sent anyone down here.'

'Well,' he said, 'my records show that in the last two months we had to issue emergency contraception to a young lady who came down here asking to be pre-scribed under your name.' I just thought, the bastard! He's sent this girl down to my doctor to discuss her contraception problems under my name. No wonder the receptionist was so curt to me when I walked in. Mr Fox, she must think, has no respect for any woman, he just uses them to satisfy his sexual needs and then chucks then down to the doctors. I explained it wasn't me but Eddie Irvine the racing driver, but the doc was having none of it, he didn't believe any of it, thought I was a complete tosser who just picked up women and used them, then dumped them on his doorstep to clear up the mess.

When I questioned Eddie about it, he just said 'Oh well, yeah, but you don't mind do you?' I mean what could I do? What do you say? I was like 'Oh yeah, well okay then.' But I didn't go back to the doctor for a while.

He has a way with the girls, which is not unrelated to his profession. We were in Mugello once where he was doing an ad with Ferrari for Shell. I turned up in the afternoon and there was a whole film crew there. There was this really sassy German lady whom I wanted to try and get to know. I couldn't decide if she was married or not, she was wearing a ring, but she didn't act married. Anyway, she had a great figure and I was checking her out because I was doing the stills for the shoot. She kept smiling over, so I thought I had a chance. Eddie turned up in his civvies and she didn't even look at him, didn't notice him at all, it was all smiles in my direction. So I thought, I'm in here, and started planning where I'd take her and how the evening would go.

Suddenly, down comes Mr Irvine dressed in his race suit and everything changed, the German lady was suddenly on fire. I never knew what a pair of red overalls could do. The power was incredible. Afterwards they went upstairs and chatted and that was that. I had to wait for him as I was going back to his house to stay the night. I was downstairs for about two hours in this pit, this garage, making small talk and waiting for him to appear. Then he comes down and says 'Okeedokee, you ready now?' and this lady came down with a smile on her face. That was the power of the whole racing driver scenario. I'd spent all day chatting her up, and all I had to do was stroll in wearing a pair of red overalls, and I'd have been fine.

Eddie's not exactly a corporate man, he's an individual. He still manages to be himself, and not become Mr Grey man doing what the sponsors expect, and I think he stands out as a more colourful, interesting character because of that. When he drives a car he fascinates me because I think it's an amazing ability to be able to do that. But like any human being he suffers from insecurities. If he doesn't win races all the time, and people put him down, he takes it quite badly. He is sensitive to criticism but he covers it up with this toy boy, playboy, mega boy image that he's got with the media. But if you take all that away, he's got quite a delicate personality.

He's not one for bullshitting. If he wants to talk, he will talk. If he doesn't, then he won't. You never have any doubts about whether he likes you or not. He's not good at pretending to feel something he doesn't. He travelled quite a lot with the racing, and when he came home to Oxford he just wanted to chill out. He still likes to just chill out. He enjoys his place in Dalkey, and I think he loves the boat. He can switch off and be with his mates, no one's staring at him and he can do what he wants to do. It's complete freedom and independence.

Like any normal guy, sometimes he can be really funny, sometimes he isn't; sometimes he has some-thing interesting to say and sometimes he doesn't. We've had some laughs together, especially in Macau. Once I walked into a lamp post while staring at some girls who were across the road and Eddie nearly split his sides. Funnily enough, he's not that great at pulling the birds. Unless they know who he is, or he's in a relaxed chilled mode, then he's shy and holds back. Instead he'd get me to go and talk to them first and see how I got on. If I did all right he'd go 'Oh shit, I've got to go and do it now.' At the same time, though, it was unusual for me to outdo him with the women. He's done well with them. He's very, very lucky and cer-tainly being a racing driver helps the situation. It's sur-

prising how many women fall for the image of the
fast, sexy playboy.

I used to go home with him for Christmas and New
Year, go and see Edmund and Kathleen and Sonia, and
it was all great and very normal. Kathleen used to
cook the meal, we'd have a really nice Christmas lunch
and sit round have a laugh and relax. It was all very
laid back – we'd all go out and get drunk, come in,
crash out or be sick in the toilet. I must have been
about 22 and he was about 25. We just had a real
laugh.

Then it changed a bit, and he'd go to Dublin bars
and everyone would be taking notice of who he was.
He liked that fact that he'd get into restaurants easily,
and maybe get free booze, but the adulation that went
with it would do his head in. He just hated having all
those people staring at him and expecting him to
entertain and perform.

I don't know what he will do after racing as he's
put everything into it. He's got an interesting mind,
but a short attention span. Maybe he just needs to get
away from Formula One when he's finished, and tease
the brain a bit, twiddle with the knobs. When the racing has gone there will be a pretty big gap to fill. I
hope after earning all that money he goes off and
enjoys it. I know he wants to sail round the world in a
yacht, which I think is a brilliant thing to do. When he
gets back from that, there's a whole world out there
and I'm sure he'll find something to do.

THE DOC

I met Eddie about five years ago. I was doing up my house in Donnybrook in Dublin at the time. I was commuting from Oxford, where I was doing clinical research, to Dublin practically every weekend and I used to bump into him a lot in the 'Library' and other places where people used to hang out. Dublin was at its peak and we were socialising with the stars. Mel Gibson had just made *Braveheart*, U2 were in the midst of the 'Achtung Baby' phase, and Tom Jones was to be found leading late night sing songs in the 'Library'. It was the 'Commitments' era and there a brilliant buzz all around.

I welcomed him to stay at my house while his cottage was being sorted out, and that's how we really became friends. It was the start of a surprising encounter. We were from totally different worlds, but shared a common involvement in the Dublin social scene. Before long I began to realise that the Irv is a bit special. For one thing, there are his attitudes. Well, I found that he's not exactly the most organised person I know. This is a guy who would invite a few friends down to stay, but he'd never organise things like who is going to sleep where, or what we're going to do. He's just says 'Right, I'm off to bed, sort yourselves out.'

The first night he moved into the cottage in Dalkey was a good example. After the 'Library' a group of us agreed to stay in the house on the first night with him. Little did we know what this house was like. Frank Cassidy, the brother of the composer Patrick Cassidy, was with us. When we got there by moonlight we found that there was no heat and no lighting, so we just had to make the best out of it. There wasn't even a torch so we couldn't find our way around. Frank was left with a mattress on the kitchen floor, and in the morning we came down to find him curled into a foetal position shivering under half a sheet. The house had been owned by Donovan in his most psychedelic phase and the walls were unbelievable. We decided that it was a good job we hadn't had a light in the house, or we would have all had nightmares!

It's not all about discomfort, though. I have had some incredible times with Eddie. We went to a big charity fashion do with all the top international models – Christy Turlington, Naomi Campbell, Karen Mulder and Yasmin le Bon – at The Point in Dublin. That was the night when Christy described him as 'cute' and I asked Naomi whether she had knitted the beautiful outfit she had worn at the end of the show. She turned to me and said icily 'No, darling I just carry them.'

Life in the company of Irv was intermittently a series of mega events. He invited me to a Rod Stewart concert once and afterwards we went to dinner in Dublin where I met Damon Hill. I found him to be really interesting and entertaining company. His insight into sports science is impressive. We had a great chat as I was writing a book on cardiac and muscle metabolism.

Irv had some characters in his circle. One of them was Derek, who used to work for Eddie, minding the house and the Dublin toys in exchange for free accommodation and a retainer. One day things didn't go quite to plan for Derek. Eddie rang him and said 'Yo, what's happening?' He quickly replied 'Oh boss, just doing some work on the jet ski,' whereupon Irv says 'Oh yeah?' as he flies over from behind Dalkey hill in the helicopter, to find Derek lying on the terrace having a beer!

The helicopter featured quite large in our lives at one stage. On one occasion we went up to a promotion in Portadown. Eddie pulled some girls in the club and wanted to go back to the Boom Boom Rooms in Bangor. As we took off in the helicopter at 1 am, we woke up the entire town. That was typical of Eddie, he just does things without thinking of the consequences. I was on the end of that forgetfulness once. We had gone to Bangor, with the agreement that he'd give me a lift back to Dublin in the helicopter the next day from his mum's house. I had to leave my car in the North for some work to be done on it. The next morning I got up early and headed to the house to join the helicopter. When I got there I found the place completely deserted. The front door was open, the back door was open, the windows were open. The oven was still on but there was no sign of the helicopter. Had there been a midnight raid I wondered? No, it was just Eddie, the brain, again.

Halfway to Dublin, Eddie suddenly said 'Yo, is someone missing? Where's the Doc?' He'd forgotten all about me, so I was left in the north of Ireland with no car and no way of getting one. Fortunately for me, his dad's mechanic, Stephen, came past the house and found me. He organised a car to get me home.

Sometimes Irv, despite the entourage, can find himself alone. I remember the first time he came back to Ireland as a Ferrari driver. He turned up in the official kit, Cerruti jacket, Gucci bag, Prada slippers, all the Italian designer gear, but was heading off to spend the night on his own in a hotel. My sister and I dragged him back to Donnybrook again so that he wouldn't be on his own at such a key moment in his life.

However, in spite of occasional forgetful behaviour, Eddie can be a clever guy. That is evident to everyone from the way he's coping with his current situation. He can measure up the scene and not allow anything to phase him. He's under pressure now, but he doesn't let it get to him. His attitude to the situation with Schumacher just highlights his laid back attitude 'Doc,' he says. 'It's not perfect, but it's something special, isn't it?' You can't drive for four years for a fantastic team like Ferrari and not be affected by it all. The expectations, driving with Schumacher, the media, being constantly in the spotlight – you can't live through that and not become more mature and more thoughtful. I think he has the ability and deserves to win the World Championship. If he does it will be good for the sport and good for his homeland.

With all the pressure this year, his boat has become an important escape route. He loves the *Anaconda* and spends lots of time on it. It is a magnificent vessel and it's kitted out with all his toys – jet skis, mountain bikes, canoes, as well as a jacuzzi, sauna etc. I crewed it up from Majorca, with his old friend Dominic. But even if Eddie is now a boat owner, he's not exactly what you'd describe as a boat man. He doesn't understand the intricacies of boats. I took him on my boat in Oxford this summer, and as we set off from the boat house I said 'Okay, cast off the ropes.' He did, and off we went. Soon we were in the middle of the river, but then we had to get to the bank where there was a photographer waiting for us. As we got near the edge of the river I said to him 'Okay, throw the rope to the guy, so we can tie up.'

'What do you mean, throw the rope, what rope?' He looked at me blankly.

'The rope you untied the boat with.' All the response I got was another blank look and then it dawned on me that he'd untied the rope and thrown it into the boat house, so we were drifting around the river with no rope to tie the boat up with. 'Another fine mess you got me in,' I said. We had to find a rope and then tie the boat up, and then get my rope from the boat house. Things are never easy with Mr Irvine but, nonetheless, life is more interesting.

Nor is Edie particularly knowledgeable about jet skis. He's brilliant at riding one, but not at looking after them. One day we went to Lake Como with his Brazilian girlfriend Christina, and he was loaned a jet ski. Off we went with the jet ski tied to the lake boat. But as we headed toward the centre a friend of the owner happened to cruise by and suddenly he's shouting 'Stop, stop.' We were confused. 'What's happening?' asks Irvine. Unbeknown to us the jet ski was sinking big time. We eventually manhandled it aboard and emptied it of water, but it wouldn't start. We returned to the owner who was very understanding and said 'Sure, you can have another one.'

We got another one and Irv rode off towards Switzerland. Christina and I eventually caught up with him and we tied the jet ski to the back of the boat. After a while we noticed that the jet ski was looking a little low in the water. Oh no, it couldn't happen a second time, or could it? Well it did and after frantic efforts to pull it out of the water, with thoughts of the *Titanic* coming to mind, we somehow got it onto the boat. Then it was back to the owner again with our tail between our legs. We thought those things were meant to float. It cost about $4000 to repair the skis, and there were red faces all round.

Irv's not got a brilliant sense of direction either. Although I have to say the direction signs in Italy don't help much. We were blasting round north Italy in a new Delta Integrale Evolutizione, a fantastic machine, on the way to Monza for a promotion. We drove up and down the motorway looking for the right turning, but couldn't find it. Eventually, we ended back at the same man in the toll booth. He couldn't believe his eyes. Here's Irvine, who drives for Ferrari, and he can't find Monza. I mean what hope is there for him, Ferrari or Italy, if he can't find the most famous circuit in the world? But I'd challenge the guy in the toll booth to find his way round Birmingham!

I like his view on life, which is to enjoy it to the full. He really does live life in the fast lane. He enjoys the money he's made, and he enjoys his toys. I don't think many rich men enjoy the rewards of their profession as much as he does. The boat, the plane, the helicopter, they are central to his life and are an important part of his relaxation and enjoyment. I have had some great times in his company and I expect they'll be many more. Once we were going round Dublin with the Jordan crew, and we saw a couple making out in a doorway, and he said to me 'Stick with me Doc, and you'll meet some fabulous birds.' I'm still waiting!

CIRO

I met Eddie at a party. We both liked the same model and we fought over her for a bit, but then after about twenty minutes, we bumped into each other and started talking. He called me, we went out to lunch and after that we were friends and started hanging out a lot together. He was living in a very small apartment and I was living with my parents, so we found this apartment in Milan and started living in it together.

It works very well as we know the same people in Milan, we like doing the same things, we like the same music, we like the same movies, so we do everything together. We argue, but then it's just the way he is, he likes to complain and he's very demanding, but I know him well enough by now to just let him get on with it. People will say yes to Eddie because they want to be close to him, but that's not my style. I like to wind him up and then have a laugh. We both do that to each other.

I work as a PR for some clubs, I organise parties,

bring in models, raise the profile of the club, get it well known amongst the in crowd, so organising parties for Eddie isn't a problem. I did actually work for Eddie for a while, but it didn't work out and we decided we'd rather be friends than employer and employee. I know he felt bad about the situation when I worked for him, and didn't know how to resolve it. He had decided to sack me, but then I talked to him and said it was better for both of us if I left, and after that our friendship carried on like before.

I still do things for him but as a friend. I kind of look after him. He always forgets things, especially the keys to the apartment, so I make sure his life runs smoothly. If he needs something, I sort it out. If his car needs fixing, I sort it out, if he has to go to the laundry to wash his clothes I do that for him. Sometimes his parents will arrive at the airport and I'll go and pick them up. They're all little things, but I enjoy doing them. He's a good friend of mine and you always look after your friends don't you?

In return he looks after me. I go to the boat or he takes me to races, and that is a thrill for me. Since I first met him three or four years ago, I have noticed the big change in his situation. Then he could walk down the street and not be bothered. Now whenever he leaves the house he has ten people following him. It is impossible for him to be left alone, and I think he finds that very hard. Sometimes he can be a bit nasty with people who follow him around, but when you get to know him he's a great guy, and if he can do something for you then he will.

COUSIN PHILIP

I remember when we were really young, we used to race go-karts at the lead mines. It was always me, Eddie and Sonia. We used to make them and then race them back. He was competitive then and he hasn't changed although he couldn't pull the girls as he wasn't the best looking guy around. We'd go out and he'd always end up single. It's a bit different now! The girls are crawling out of the woodwork to get to him. But back then he wasn't a pretty picture, but we always got on well. We always used to get him to drive the car home after a night out, because he wouldn't drink and he wasn't going to pull, so it seemed to be an ideal situation.

We shared a place in London when he went to there to race, and we managed to get arrested one day. We were coming back from London and were at a round-about. He was going fast, but not that fast, and I looked across and saw a police car. We turned right and headed back into a housing estate, but the police were now chasing us. We could hear sirens coming from everywhere, it was like *Miami Vice*, there must have been six or seven police cars surrounding us. We got pulled over and he was done for reckless driving.

I have a great time with Eddie, I go on the boat, go to clubs and to races, but I wouldn't swop his lifestyle for anything. I'd hate the attention that his job brings him. He can't do anything without people knowing about it, or staring at him, and I wouldn't want that.

I find it amazing that he's driving for Ferrari and going for the World Championship. In 1987 we were in

England and he was driving a Formula Ford. I could never have predicted that he'd go this far. We knew he was good from the start but we never realised he'd go all the way to the top, and maybe even win the most fantastic prize of all – the World Championship. It would be brilliant if he won that, brilliant for him, our families, his friends and everyone who's supported him along the way and also good for his homeland. For Ireland to have a World Champion would be absolutely fantastic.

CHAPTER 5

Canada and France

I did a lot of testing the week before Canada at Fiorano, so much I was dizzy by the end of the day. It was a new record for Fiorano, in terms of lap times and in the number of laps completed in one day. The fastest lap was 1 min. 1 sec. and we did something like 135 laps. For three days we were there from nine in the morning until nine at night.

I was pretty happy on the Friday before the Canada race. We made some good set up changes, followed by some bad ones, and finally another good one. My last lap on Friday should have been my best but I used too much of the kerb at one point. I had no problem with the brakes, but this is a track where you have to check the wear rate very carefully. The tyres worked well, but as usual here, the track was dirty in the morning and improved lap by lap.

The car was going really well and I thought I could have got Pole rather than third on the grid. I left my big effort for the last run of the qualifying session, but my mate Jean Alesi had the yellow flags out at the first corner. I had to back off, and the tenth of a second or so that I lost might have cost me Pole. It was a shame not to be on the front row, because it would have been nice to have kept Mika behind.

At the start of the race I was looking after the brakes and trying to go as fast as I could without pushing the car too much. When I did start to push, the safety car came out in response to Villeneuve's accident. If that hadn't happened I think I could have gone on to win as I was at a really good point. I got a message that the safety car was coming out when I'd just gone past the entrance to the pits, otherwise I would have taken advantage of this situation and gone in for a change of tyres.

DC and I then had a bit of a coming together. He seemed to come into the pits overtaking the pace car which was going into the pits, then I thought he drove through a red light on his exit from the pits. I felt that cost me two points for sure as I reckon I would have finished second otherwise, rather than my final position of third. DC got a run at me and when we got to the corner we were side by side. But he went very wide there, so I turned into the next corner, alongside him, and his front wing clipped my rear wheel. Afterwards he said to me that I didn't leave him any room, but I just replied that if I'd given him any room we'd have had to drive into the grandstands rather than round the corner. I've got to say I think one of our main objectives is to keep the cars from travelling through the grandstands if at all possible.

I got to have some fun with Johnny Herbert after that. Johnny was much slower than me and I went down the inside of him. We both braked on the limit and I was on the dirt on the inside. I could have tried to make the corner, but I might have lost it completely so I went straight on. I don't know what happened to Johnny, except that he seemed to lose a lot of time, too. I don't know if he got through the corner or followed me over on the grass. He might have complained about my behaviour but Formula One isn't for kids. I tried to overtake then, since it was my only chance as the Stewart is faster on the straights.

Anyway, I think it's good to have a bit of controversy in the race, that's why people come to watch it. If you have a procession of cars it gets boring and people switch off. The whole point of Formula One is that it is a great spectacle. Of course you've got to have the awful days just to show off the good days, but as in any sport, the interest is in the unexpected. If every golfer stood on the green and put the ball into the hole with one putt, it would become tedious, but it is the exceptional shot or the unexpected blunder that gives it that rush of excitement. It's the same in Formula One. The fans are waiting for a great overtaking manoeuvre or a crash, or, of course, for one of the McLarens to break down.

There's got to be an element of uncertainty. If you had Adrian Newey and Michael Schumacher at the same team, I think it would kill off Formula One, so we're quite lucky that Adrian's wife doesn't want to live abroad, or that Michael Schumacher makes more bucks at Ferrari. If the two of them got together then I think Bernie could pack up and go home. It would be a one team race. Maybe occasionally the little guy would come along and win, but most of the time it would be very predictable.

There's always pressure to perform and perform well. That's why you get drugs in sport, there's always pressure to go faster, do better. I'm dead against drugs and the Ben Johnson incident was a serious disappointment to me. I had been very impressed by his time and I remember watching him in Seoul and thinking that this was a great moment in sport – this guy just smashing the time barriers, this superman who could do something that the experts said was impossible. In fact, as we later found out, it was impossible. It was down to drugs, and I think that took a lot away from athletics. In fact, athletics as a whole has lost credibility in the last few years. It seems as if whenever someone does an amazing time, the next thing we hear they've been caught with drugs. Every time I see someone winning now I think to myself that he's probably got the best chemist.

I'm lucky in that I have Sonia and she always checks and double checks any medicines I'm taking. I tend to get colds and take Lemsip for that, but she always makes sure it is within the FIA regulations. I'd take part in an anti-drugs campaign if I was asked and I think drugs are the biggest destroyer of youth today. They go to the clubs and take ecstasy and end up dead. What a waste of life. There are stories every day in the papers that drugs like ectasy kill, but the kids still take it. I don't think it's cool or sophisticated, I think it just shows you're behaving pretty stupidly. I've been offered drugs by people out and about but it doesn't interest me, and I don't think it is a clever thing to do.

We don't really have major drug problem in Formula One in terms of the drivers. I can't think of any drug that would enhance performance and give you an edge. It's not a physical type of thing like athletics. But there is cocaine use amongst certain people who want to party. I party with my own energy and think it's pretty pathetic to take drugs to stay awake. However, if someone came to me and offered me a safe drug that would give me an edge over my competitors and win me the World Championship, I'd think for a moment before refusing. The desire to win is overwhelming and can mean people take risks. It is right for the authorities to clamp down and throw people out of their sport if found out, but I can understand that desperation to win.

I had a nasty shock awaiting me when I'd finished celebrating my third place at Canada. Michael had made a mistake and gone into the wall, and had understandably wanted to get away. But getting in and out isn't that easy. I'd planned my escape with the precision of an SAS raid. I had to get a connecting Aer Lingus flight from New York to Dublin that night and I was determined to make it. Everything was organised – I had a helicopter slot out of the circuit to Montreal airport and then the private jet waiting for me to whisk me to New York and from there to Dublin. Easy peasy, we had it all planned. There was no way I was going to miss that flight.

But I'd reckoned without Michael, who rapidly left the circuit, grabbed the first helicopter slot which happened to be mine, and disappeared into the distance, leaving me stranded. As a result I was 30 minutes late leaving and arrived in New York with only 30 minutes to spare to get the flight to Dublin. Just to help matters along Aer Lingus had sold my Club Class ticket to Dublin so I ended up cramped in the back of the plane. It's funny how things can bring you back down to earth. A few hours earlier I'd been celebrating third place and my team had been really happy. Michael had been the unhappy one, having made a mistake and gone out of the race. But I had ended up crammed in economy. Life is funny sometimes, just when you think you're a hero something happens to remind you that you're an ordinary bloke after all! I very much felt Number Two to Michael both on and off the track, in victory and defeat.

But I was back in Europe and my next destination was France. Magny Cours is in the middle of the country, near a town called Nevers, which was quite appropriate bearing in mind the débâcle that was to be the French Grand Prix.

The real disadvantage of competing at Magny Cours is that it is difficult to get to by public transport, but my plane, which is a Falcon 10, comes into its own in such situations. In the old days I would have had to get up at the crack of dawn for a late afternoon meeting. If I'd been in Dublin then I would have had to leave on the first flight to London, connect from London to Paris on one of the scheduled flights, and then drive for four hours to get to the track. Alternatively I could have taken the chartered flight out of London to Nevers. Either way you look at it, it's hassle and it involves queuing, my least favourite activity.

I hate wasting time, I hate losing even a minute of my life, and one of the biggest time wasters is using commercial aircraft. You have to queue to get to the airport, queue to get your ticket, queue to check in, queue through security, queue through passport control, queue to get on the bus to get on the plane, and then queue to get on the plane. Then when you arrive you have to queue to get off the plane, queue to get through passport control, and so on all the way through to driving away from the airport.

At the same time this involves suffering from my second least favourite activity – people gawping at me. Get on a plane and you are stuck while you have to listen to someone tell you their life story, or tell you how they would have taken the fourth corner at Silverstone, and why can't Ferrari win the Championship with all the money they spend? You can't get away, and in the end you have to be rude and pretend to go to sleep.

My plane has more than paid for itself. I can board at about eleven o'clock on the Thursday before the race and be at the circuit at Magny Cours just after lunch. I can also have meetings or entertain sponsors in complete privacy. If I ever decided to upgrade the plane, I'd have a Falcon 50, which is the big brother of my Falcon 10. It costs about $12 million and has a longer range. It can do short runs to New York, and nothing touches it performance-wise. But to be honest I don't really need it, and I can't justify the increase in cost. It would just be extravagant and that's against my nature.

Helicopters are also a love of mine. The first time I went in one I couldn't believe how mega they are. The freedom of movement in the air is incredible and I'm very glad I learnt how to fly one. I did buy my own helicopter but now I just hire one when I need it in Ireland. My mum and dad's neighbours don't seem to mind the noise of it landing in the back garden, so it's convenient for me to nip backwards and forwards to see them when I want to.

Magny Cours turned out to be a strange race. In 1998 we had achieved a one-two finish for Ferrari, with Michael first and me second, but this year wasn't going to be quite the same. The weather didn't help – it was raining and overcast and difficult to judge whether to put wet weather tyres on or not.

It turned out to be a major tactical error not to go out early in qualifying. By the time I was on the track I was aquaplaning everywhere. On my last run, when I was heading for a better time, I came across a car going slowly through the chicane and I spun trying to avoid him. My power steering had failed as I left the pits on my last run, so that didn't help, either. I also lost time as I was weighed twice by the scrutineers. They can do this anytime we come in but it stops us reporting straight back to our engineers in the pits, and also from measuring the tyre temperatures.

Nevertheless, it's part of the regulations, and we all run the risk of getting stopped. All the same, seventeenth was not a great grid position, whichever way you look at it!

I had a lousy start in the race as well, as I was in neutral and lost time having to select first. I knew it was going to rain, so I decided to take it carefully at first to save the tyres. I also knew I'd have a good chance to pick people off in the rain. Once the start was out of the way I got up speed and started picking off cars. I must have overtaken about eighteen when I radioed the team saying 'Pits, pits.' But it was a bad stop, with nearly forty seconds lost while they tried to find the tyres, which weren't ready. We analysed this hiccup afterwards and changes were made. In the future the pit crew were to sit in the garage in a half moon shape so they would be ready for the pit stops and everyone would be better prepared.

After this bad stop I then spun behind the safety car. But the car was okay and I overtook about another eighteen cars and found I could catch up with Michael quite easily – although not overtake him, obviously – and we finished fifth and sixth. It was a shame because the cars performed well and we hadn't taken advantage of that. I could have done a one stop race as we started with a lot of fuel, but it just wasn't our day. I think we missed a great opportunity to get points and I predicted that this race would come back and haunt us later in the year. In this game every point counts.

Heinz Harald Frentzen won, and I was pleased for him. He's going well this year with Jordan having had a nightmare with Williams. He was second in Australia when I won, third in Brazil, fourth in Monaco and finally won in France.

If it had been a dry race I think we would have finished first and second, as we'd prepared the cars so well. We were certainly faster than the McLarens. This time it was Eddie Jordan's turn to have a joke. He came up to me and said 'Here's the first of the losers,' to get me back for my identical comment in Australia! However this time he added I could be a winner next year with him!

I think one of the common misconceptions about me is that I'm accident prone and inconsistent, but if you actually analyse at my results, I'm one of the most consistent drivers in the Championship. In fact, I've always been consistent and if you look at the year before I joined Ferrari, I was the only driver who didn't crash out of a race that year, so I don't think the accusation holds water. In 1996 the car was a disaster, but in 1997 I started to come back and in 1998 I had eight podium appearances. Not bad for a number two driver.

After France we had a major tyre test at Silverstone. On my way there I dropped in to see my old friend Bruce Milani Gallieni and to help him launch his scooter business, BMG scooters, which is based in Richmond. Bruce has been a good friend for a long time, and he also provides the London market with luxury and high performance cars. I've always loved scooters, especially my favourite the Piaggio, and so it was fun for my girlfriend Anouk and I to pop into London for a couple of days' relaxation. It's easy to get round London on two wheels and with a helmet on, no one recognises you, either. It beats the traffic and the parking problem in one go, so when I'm in town I hop on a scooter and zip around the place. I use scooters to get in and out of the circuits as well.

We stayed in Notting Hill, and after the launch we went to the pub and downed a few pints. It is great to be able to act like an normal person and go into a pub without getting hassled. As it turned out, this was to be my last quiet moment for quite a long time.

Testing is not my favourite occupation, but it's like another day in the office, you get down to it, and do the job in hand. It's a misconception to say that Michael is great at testing and I'm not. I've had a lot more input in set up than people think. DC remarked that Ferrari were missing Michael's technical input and feed back when I took over as number one. Basically, Michael is an amazingly talented driver, but I don't think test driving was his particularly strong point. He is so talented that he'll just drive through a problem. Sometimes that much natural talent can be a hindrance when you're testing small changes in a car. In 1997 he tried out the biggest aerodynamic step forward we'd ever had at Ferrari. He didn't like it and they put it back in the truck. I didn't test it then as he just said it was awful, but I tested it the following week and went half a second faster. The biggest step forward we've ever made and it was sitting in the back of the truck at Nurburgring!

Undeterred, we eventually got him to try it again and he found he went half a second faster, so naturally he used it on the car. Michael was like that when he first came to Ferrari and didn't want the two pedal system which I'd been using, initially saying he wanted to stay with the three pedal, until he found out he could go quicker and that it was the way forward. Sometimes I feel Michael can be resistant to trying anything new. Occasionally you have to go with the flow and just do it, see what it's like and then decide if it is worth it or not.

It was the same when we started testing this year. Michael drove the car for the first three weeks and then I drove it at Mugello, and I thought 'Shit, there's something very strange at the rear end.' I came in and complained about it and found they'd been testing for three weeks with too stiff a rear end. They softened it off and the car then felt fantastic.

Some people have cited his testing at Benetton as an example of his brilliance on the test track. He went one and a half seconds quicker than Johnny at one test, and so instantly became the test maestro. I can't talk about Benetton, but I know what goes on at Ferrari and it isn't as simple as that. I'm not taking anything away from his brilliance on the track, he is a genius, but that doesn't mean he can automatically excel at everything else.

But, to give him his due, Michael is highly motivated and he has the ability to get everyone working to his tune, which is a very good quality to have in a sport like Formula One. No one can accuse him of not putting in the hours; sometimes, it's difficult to get him away from the track. Ferrari is a place where a lot of time is wasted. They love wasting time in Italy, people talk and pontificate all day. I hate that, I like to just get on with the job. I'm not particularly talkative, Pete and Ciro can talk all day, but I can't. I'd like to change that about myself and become a little more communicative. Jean Todt knows that I don't like speaking on the telephone, as I just can't be bothered. In the beginning, he wanted me to call him all the time, but now he only calls me if there is a reason to call, and we are all happier with that arrangement.

If you've got a passion for stress, as well as time-wasting there is no better place to be than Ferrari. You can wallow in it all day. Pressure, pressure, pressure. I must admit my knowledge of racing is ten times what it was before I joined Ferrari, and my technique is a lot better. I used to fly into corners, brake as late as possible, and only then worry about the rest, how I was going to get through the corner. Now I've learnt from Michael, who is outstanding at getting the most from the car, I take the corner in a smoother, more thought-out manner and it works – you go faster. Perhaps Michael and I have taken things from each other. I am better at spotting what's not right with the car and he's been a maestro at teaching the finer points of motor racing, and how to squeeze that extra few tenths from the car by driving it a little differently. And there's no doubt that when push came to shove at the end of the season, he was right there behind me. He's a great team-mate – my dream number two.

I would say you are at your peak as a driver at 33 because you understand what's important. You might not be as brave or stupid as you were at 20, but overall you do a better job. I think you understand more about what you need, you understand more about particular circuits. It is a continuous learning process. From this point of view I don't think I'm going to get any faster at driving. I've learnt things in the last couple of years, like how to attack certain corners, and also about the set up of the car so it is just as I want it. For some on the circuit driving is an intellectual process, for others it's just gut reaction. As far as I'm concerned, I'm always thinking about where to brake and where to turn in. At the same time I'm obviously thinking about strategy, and working out where the other guys are in the race. You also have to bear in mind how the car's going and the performance of the tyres. You might also be looking at how you can change your line to help make the car better, because you can't alter the set up during a race. In effect, you're always trying to improvise during a race. It's an ongoing process, and at 33 you have the experience and are still young enough to have quick reactions.

Combined with this you have to have judgement. You're right on the limit when driving and that's what it's all about. That's why drivers who go on the circuit for the first time always go off the track. They're either massively slow or they spin off because they haven't yet got the judgement that come from a combination of talent and experience. The experienced driver also occasionally has an accident, or a lucky escape, but in general racing is quite a calm experience. Most problems are not the fault of the driver, anyway. The car is now so complicated that it's a wonder it goes at all. It's a very complex system and there are a thousand ways it can go wrong. Long gone are the days when you'd just jack it up, change the tyres, bolt on an engine and go.

I find that I talk to myself about everything, especially on test days when there isn't the same pressure. That is when you have a lot more time, so there are more things in your head. Sometimes during a race you can drift off, if the guy in front of you is far ahead and the guy behind you is also far away. Sometimes I'll think about the next race, the Championship points, or even where I'm going after the race. It is quite easy to drive the car – you just sit there and go into automatic pilot where you don't really think about anything. Like dancing, you're just in the flow. Sometime driving is fantastic, sometimes it's just a job. The pressure of a result now is more important than it was before, so the enjoyment factor goes down. Even if you've enjoyed driving the car, unless you've got a result in the race it doesn't count for anything.

Sitting in the car is not a comfortable experience even if you do have the type of seat you want. The car is made as small as possible, because the smaller something is the faster it will go through the air. When you get into the car you feel pretty claustrophobic, because it is so tight. As you drive your knees are hitting the monocock and your head is hitting the head rest behind you. The most tiring thing, though, is moving around. Even if you try to make sure you don't move, when you're pulling 4-5G your body moves whatever you do. You can multiply your body weight by five when you're braking. It is also very noisy, even with ear plugs it is deafening. I hate the noise, which might sound odd coming from a F1 driver, but there it is. I hate baby noise, but I hate engine noise as much, or rather I hate the noise of the V10 engine. The V12 was beautiful but the V10 is a horrible sound, the five cylinders sound unbalanced and unnatural. Bernie should ban V10 engines. The first thing I'll do at Jaguar is get the V12 back!

It is difficult to explain the fun of driving these type of cars. What's the fun in dancing? It's the same sort of thing. It looks a ridiculous thing to do, standing in the middle of the dance floor, jumping up and down like a lunatic, but we're getting fun from that. I can't explain why but we do. It's the same with driving a Formula One car. I don't see it as a thrill any more, but it's a nice feeling nonetheless. It's the same as when I ride the jet ski. I just love the feeling of trying to do things that are difficult, and the sensation of sliding and trying to control the car. It's a great sense of achievement when you've done a really good lap, or had a really good race. Overtaking is amazing when you manage to do it. Canada was great for that. I was pleased with coming third, but the buzz was overtaking all those cars. I had a lot of fun because, the more difficult it is to overtake, the more pleasure you get out of it. You also get more pleasure overtaking certain drivers rather than others, as you know it will hurt them more.

Although I didn't know it at the time, overtaking was going to be a major issue at Silverstone, and the result of Michael's overtaking manoeuvre during that first lap would also give me the biggest opportunity of my life – the chance to go for the World Championship. When it comes down to it, that is what it's all about.

CHAPTER 6

Women and Children

EDMUND SENIOR

Being involved in racing myself, I wanted to call Eddie 'Stirling Moss Irvine', but I was persuaded not to by the family, and it's probably good I didn't. You can imagine what that would be like for him now! Eddie's first grand prix was probably when he was about four or five, when we used to spend our summer holidays at the British Grand Prix. The kids would always get into the track without paying, as I didn't believe in paying for kids as they were the future. I can remember one year Eddie slept beside the track all night so he wouldn't have to pay to get in. He was just like any kid and we would pick up buntings and banners. If it wasn't nailed down we'd take it with us, and it would be hanging from the two trees we had. One year we had a John Player Special banner that must have been thirty foot long. It hung from the trees for a long time.

I used to drive single-seater cars, but I never ever thought of becoming a Formula One driver. For me it was just having fun, and I thought it would be the same for Eddie. It was just something for him to do, that's how it got started. Then it just progressed, from here to England, from England to Europe and Europe to Japan and then back again. It's incredible to think of how it has all happened. He had wanted a motor cycle, but I thought they were dangerous, so we swapped an old Ford Capri for a Ford Crossle with the idea that I'd race it and he could play about in it. But I did one race in it and didn't like it, so I said to Eddie 'You drive it and race it and I'll look after it.'

The deal was that he'd work unpaid down the scrap yard I had, and that would pay for his racing. We didn't buy new tyres, other drivers would give us their old tyres. The money we did spend would probably have gone a long way towards the house, but Kathleen never seemed to mind. She just accepted it and got on with it. Eddie worked seven days a week for no money to go racing. When he went to England a lot of the other drivers stayed in hotels, but he slept in the back of a truck with the mechanics and the car. I think it was good training for him. If you have to work for it, and rough it a bit, then I think you appreciate success more. I always taught Eddie to earn money and work for it. I don't approve of young kids going on the dole, there's always work to be done, and if you're fit then you should work to earn a living.

That said, I've always tried to support him when he couldn't help himself. When he needed a new racing car, because we had got a good deal with a new manufacturer, I needed about £5,000 so he could have the car. At the time I didn't have 25 quid, so I went down to see the bank manager and said that Kathleen wanted a new kitchen. This got us an overdraft, and we used that to buy the car. When through Eddie Jordan we got the chance to drive in an English Formula Ford team, they needed £10,000, so off I went to see the bank manager again!

People think Eddie is super-confident but he's only confident in certain things. If he's going to do something and it looks a bit dangerous, then he'll weigh it up before he goes into it. When Eddie was little,

Kathleen and I were sitting at Bangor swimming pool, watching him. He climbed to the top of the dive board – he can only have been about six at the time – and looked over the end to see if he was going to dive off. In all he must have been up there about three-quarters of an hour trying to make up his mind whether he was going to dive off or not. I can remember that Dick Milligan, the Irish Rugby player, was there as he'd broken his leg and was doing some water training. He was watching Eddie and shouting at him to dive, but he wouldn't do it. Finally, after thinking about it for ages, he did dive off. Everyone was watching him and willing him to do it. But that's Eddie, he weighs things up; he's not a natural risk taker, he likes to know the odds are stacked in his favour.

Motor racing is dangerous, and the part I don't like is the start. I always get butterflies at that moment. Kathleen is the same, she'll wander about at the start and then gradually make her way back to the hospitality suite and we'll watch the race from there. After the start I'm fairly relaxed as regards an accident. If you do have an accident then Formula One is well equipped to deal with it – they have some of the best medical facilities in the world.

Eddie has this reputation for being wild, but he was a good kid and rarely got into trouble. I do remember when he was about six or seven he climbed up a tree and got stuck, then a neighbour climbed up after him and got stuck as well. I came home from work to find two people stuck up a tree, so I had to go up and get both of them down.

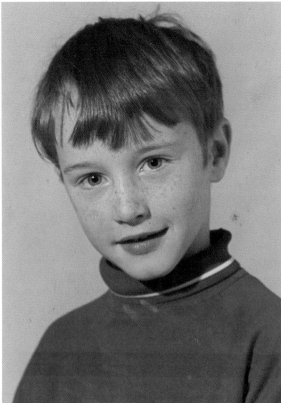

Man and Boy.
(Left) 1971,
(below) 1999 © Rose/ Sutton
◀▼

The family with Grandad Irvine.

One of my first races, aged 17, Kirkston.

◄ Like father,
like son.
Dad racing,
1978.

► Me, Bruce
and a Gilera
Runner, 1999.

◄ Anouk and I, 1999.

◄ Zoe
© Peter Fox/MSM

Maria, Zoe & I, 1999. © Peter Fox/MSM ▲

▲ Lunch on the Anaconda; (l-r) Zoe, Maria, me, Dad, Sonia and Mum.
© Peter Fox/MSM

A few of my toys.
© Peter Fox/MSM
◀▼

Jean Todt with Michael and I, celebrating at Monaco 1997. © Sutton ▲

Two years later at Canada 1999, the picture tells a different story. © Sutton ▲

▼ The start of Australia 1999, and the start of a new stage in my racing career. © Sutton

◄
On the podium and
loving every minute,
Australia 1999. © Sutton

▲ Team concentration at Monaco 1999.
© Flavio Mazzi

◄

My manager Enrico and I have
a pre-race discussion at San
Marino 1999. © Flavio Mazzi

Victory is sweet,
Australia 1999.
© Sutton Motorsport
Images

▲ The crucial Grand Prix, Silverstone 1999. © Flavio Mazzi

▼ Pit-stop, Austria 1999. © Flavio Mazzi

Mutual appreciation after my second Grand Prix win, ▲
Luca Baldisserri and I, Austria 1999. © Flavio Mazzi

The Ferrari Team in full, triumphant force, Austria 1999. © Flavio Mazzi ▼

▶

My sister Sonia
and I pre-race,
Hockenheim,
Germany 1999.
© Sutton

Ferrari at Monza,
Italy 1999. © Sutton ▼

Post-race mayhem, Hockenheim, Germany 1999. © Sutton & Flavio Mazzi ▲▼

▲ At home in County Down, Northern Ireland. © Sutton

It's a hard life.
Silverstone (right)
and Hungary, 1999.
© Tommy Hilfiger &
© Flavio Mazzi
▼▶

Snowboarding in Italy.
© Sutton

Motor racing was a part of all our lives, and it has
continued like that. It was a family thing, Kathleen,
myself, and my father would go to the race. We used
to have a lot of fun, there'd be maybe 20 or 30 people
queuing up to get hamburgers from our old motor
home. We met a lot of people, and they're still friends.
I think it was more fun then, as there wasn't the pressure. In fact it was fun right up until Eddie got into a
works team in England. Formula One is not so much
fun, it's a very intense weekend. We're lucky if we get
to speak to Eddie for five minutes in the Paddock.
There are so many meetings, sponsorship appearances
to make, and other demands that the drivers don't get
time to socialise.

All in all, now that he's famous, we can't spend so
much time as a family and I miss not having time to
chat as father and son. Even when he comes home,
people call up at the house and you can't just turn
them away. We take out a camper van to the grands
prix and he used to be able to come down for something to eat, as did Sonia. But people got to know and
it became like a peep show. I suppose that's the price
of fame. Nowadays a lot of the fans don't believe
we're Eddie's parents when we arrive at the camp site
for the grand prix and park up. They think we should
be staying in a big hotel, but I like the camp site as it's
more relaxing.

Whenever he goes to a grand prix it's work for him
but for Kathleen and I it's a holiday so we try not to
get in the way. I suppose it would have been like
someone coming down and watching me working in

the garage. But in the winter we do a get a chance to really relax with him. We spent a week on the boat last year with him off the Italian coast, and it was a great week – Eddie was able to relax and go on his jet-ski, and we were able to be together as a family.

Kathleen and I met in a dance hall and wrote to each other while I was in Canada for two years. She had worked out that I was fond of a drink and a night out with my mates but I won her round in the end. We married in 1962 and toured Ireland for our honeymoon and fished a lot. I seem to remember Kathleen caught a good deal more than me. Sonia and Eddie followed very quickly. On the night he was born I was on the night shift, which finished at 7 in the morning. Sonia was about eighteen months old, and when Eddie was born we were delighted to have one of each. We had very little money, living from week to week. If I had the money I'd just go and spend it, so Kathleen managed the money. It was hard work, especially with a young family, but she never complained when I spent money on motor racing. It could have gone into the house and maybe made her life easier but she was always right behind us. Eddie's always liked cars. When he was a baby, I'd sometimes take him for a ride in the car if he couldn't sleep, and he'd always drop off.

Sometimes I think back to those days and how it used to be. We were in Monaco this year on Eddie's boat in the harbour and I was sitting drinking champagne with Kathleen. We were with a few friends and I said to them 'The first time I came here was with my brother-in-law in the car, when we drove about 1500 to

2000 miles from Durham. We drove all day and all night and into the car park, and then slept on the tarmac.' That's how we spent the weekend – sleeping on the tarmac and watching the race. Compared to that it was hard to believe that we were now in the harbour along with all the rich people and that Eddie was here as a driver, competing at the top.

Eddie's success has made our lives more interesting. We've travelled all over the world and met so many people, and made many friends, and not just because of our connection with Eddie – most didn't even know who we were. Now we can travel all over the world, to Australia, South Africa and Germany, and look up friends. We'd never have been able to do that if Eddie hadn't got into Formula One. It's definitely improved our quality of life, and I hope it continues.

Now that Eddie is so high profile, we are getting recognised more and more. The result is that people will come and talk to us, and they'll want their photograph taken with us and autographs. I have to admit it gets a bit on top of us at times. We were out for a meal in a bar recently and several people came over. It may have been an interruption, but they're fans and I always try and remember when I was like that, so I try and give them as much time as possible and give them photographs.

After the race we normally get the trophy. In Budapest recently we were staying at Beckett's, so we got the trophy in the bar and all the fans in there got their photograph taken with it. People enjoy that because it's not something they'd normally be able to do.

Zoe is my daughter. Her mother, Maria Drummond and I met when I was racing in Formula 3 in 1988. Without doubt Maria has been one of the biggest influences in my life and one of the most important relationships I've had. She has watched me move from being one of a group of racing drivers, struggling for recognition, to being in contention for the World Championship. Despite all the pressures of Formula One and living apart, we have an enormous amount of respect for each other. And my lovely Zoe enriches both our lives.

Maria

Eddie and I met in Macau when he was competing in a race there. My first impression was 'Oh, he's a good looking guy.' I thought he was Italian. Eddie's dad, Big Ed, was there too, so my friend asked him if I could have a photograph taken with Eddie, and Big Ed took the photo. Three days later, I went to a club, met up with some friends and he was there dancing, and seemed very happy. He came up to me and kissed me, which surprised me but I thought 'Oh he's just having a good time, it doesn't mean anything, I'd better not get him into trouble.' I didn't know if he had a girlfriend or not.

We were friends for a whole year, and he kept calling me from Europe, which was a surprise, as I didn't expect it – racing drivers have that love-them-and-leave-them reputation. I thought he must really like me, even though at the time I was going out with someone else. He used to say to me 'Why are you going out with that bloke, when you could have me with you?' I thought he was just joking.

A year later I went to Europe, so I met up with him again and things started from there, because by then I'd split up with my boyfriend, and Eddie and I had started to talk more often. When he got the opportunity to race in Japan in 1991, or stay in Europe, he took the option to race in Japan, and that was great for us and for our relationship. He just kept flying backwards and forwards between Japan and Macau to see me. I was working in the tax office in Macau, but we still had plenty of time to be together. From his behaviour I was convinced that he must love me. I wouldn't have been nearly as persistent or constant, and I was really impressed by it.

He was different from the other boys I met. He was really cute in his own way, and always made me laugh. I remember saying to him 'You're very conceited,' then he called up one day and said 'Oh guess what, there's another girl who says I'm very conceited, so I guess you're right then!' He was always different. People say he's very confident and quite arrogant, but I think he's quite shy and keeps his emotions locked in, especially with people he doesn't know very well. When he meets new people he's quite quiet and this is sometimes mistaken for arrogance. He only opens up and relaxes with people once he knows them. I have to say that we were always very relaxed with each other. Sometimes racing in Japan wasn't that much fun for him – he was a long way from home, a long way from his friends and family back in Northern Ireland – but when he came to see me it was like coming to see a

good friend, for both of us. For me racing drivers were
no big deal. It's the person that counts and he knows
that, he knows when people are genuine.

I can't say he was the perfect boyfriend, he was just
so messy. I'd go out to work and come home to find
bits of newspaper strewn all over the floor, and I'd
have to clear up the whole room. But I think he liked
me pampering him, and I loved pampering, it was my
way of showing I loved him. I would wash his hair
and then I would dry it with my hands, just scrunch-
ing it around until it was dry. I would give him facials
and massages and try and help him relax, and also do
things like peel his grapes, and remove the pips before
giving them to him to eat. I'd spoil him but he just
loved it. I'm very tactile and he loves to be touched.
He was also very romantic. He would send me letters
and flowers, and that was wonderful. He would also
travel round the world with a bag of coins so he could
ring me from wherever he was.

We really tried to make it work, but I knew it would
be doomed when he went into Formula One. The
lifestyle went up a gear and there was so much temp-
tation. I didn't trust him with women and I wanted a
true relationship with no pretence. In addition to that
you've got the constant travelling, so it was always
going to be difficult. I just made the decision. It was
me who took the initiative to end it. Eddie believed he
could make it work, but I wasn't sure. At the end of
1993 he had asked me to marry him, and we had started looking for houses together in Ireland. By 1994,
when he was in his first year with Jordan, I knew it

wasn't going to work and we broke up at the end of the year.

I knew that Formula One was his big chance and it would lead him into a different life. I thought that giving him his freedom would be the best thing I could do. In hindsight I don't know if that was the right decision, but I'll never know that.

But after we split up we remained good friends. Then Zoe came along. I went on holiday to visit Big Ed and Big Kate, Eddie's mum in Northern Ireland, and to see some friends. I wasn't expecting to see Eddie and that was not the purpose of my trip. Eddie's family have always been very important to me. My parents are dead so I have adopted Big Ed and Big Kate as my parents. Eddie's paternal granddad had died that year so I thought I'd go and see them as I was on my way to Portugal. I'm half Chinese, a quarter Portuguese and quarter Scottish, so I have quite a few places to look up my ancestors!

I arrived at Big Ed's and, next thing, Eddie's helicopter is landing in the back garden and he's there and the pilot is saying 'I didn't know we were staying the night.' Straightaway I thought 'There you go, there's Eddie for you.' I guess what happened happened because we still had feelings for each other.

There was no question of me not keeping Zoe. I felt I could cope, I was 29 and had lived life and felt emotionally secure enough to bring up a child and find the strength to be a single mother. When I told Eddie he was shocked because he didn't know how to deal with it. He knew he couldn't be there for Zoe, or for me, and I don't think he knew how to handle the situation. Although he now adores Zoe, at first it was hard for him to take it all in. I then told his parents, in fact I told them before Eddie did, and they said they'd support whatever decision I made.

Zoe was born on 27 March and to start with we all just took one step at a time to learn and to cope with it all. I went to stay with friends in Australia. We kept it very quiet not because there was anything to be ashamed of, but because with Eddie's career, I thought it would be just easier to keep it private. I didn't, and still don't want to be in the spotlight. Zoe's a great child – she was a really easy baby and she's an easy child. She never cried when she woke up as a baby, she'd just lie in her cot and smile at me until I played with her or fed her.

I've never lost contact with Eddie or his family, and having Zoe has just strengthened that bond between us. Just because I stopped going out with Eddie, didn't mean I stopped seeing his family. Sonia lived with me for a while in Kent, and they've all been a big part of my life for ten years now. I've got to know them well and they're really good to me. I guess I'm lucky they've been so supportive.

Big Ed and Big Kate come over and see us on their way to the races, and I go with Zoe to Ireland, so we used to see quite a lot of each other. Zoe loves her grand parents, and when they're not around she'll suddenly say 'I want my granny and grandpa' and she'll start crying. Once I had to call them before nine in the morning as she woke up and cried for them.

Now that I've moved back to Macau it isn't quite so easy, but we'll make sure we all see each other. Eddie has a private plane so it's not as though he has to save for two years before he can come out and see us. I just have to make a life for myself. Eddie has made sure we're both looked after financially, and Big Ed and Big Kate have always supported me emotionally.

Zoe is an exact combination of both of us. She has Eddie's face shape and all my features. She's got eyes the same shape as mine, but they're blue like Eddie's. She has my nose and lips and his chin. In character I guess she is like him rather than me. She's stubborn and quite shy, taking a while to get to know people before she trusts them. She also has Eddie's delayed emotional response mechanism. She'll pretend that nothing bothers her and won't show emotion at the time, and then she'll show it after the event. For example, when she leaves her granny and granddad she won't appear to be bothered, acting as though she's just going down the road for a cup of tea. Then, a few hours later when we've landed at London airport, she'll get really upset and suddenly realise she won't see them for a while. Just like her dad, it's all hidden.

Also like her dad, she's a bit of a daredevil and loves speed. Recently Zoe saw a picture of Eddie when he was young and she said 'It's me, it's me.' They are very alike. I'm glad she looks like him. She is a wonderful reminder of a very good relationship. It's like having part of Eddie forever.

Eddie was a bit scared of the situation, so he didn't see much of her as a baby, and he hates babies' crying.

Also he was very busy – it was his first year with Ferrari and he was away a lot, so he didn't have time to get to know Zoe. I moved to England with her when she was six months old, and we lived in Chislehurst in Kent. When Eddie and she were first together, Zoe was rather scared of him and it took her quite a long while to get used to the idea of having Eddie around. He didn't know what to do with a baby, either, so it was a learning process both ways.

Now they are developing a great relationship and she definitely knows who her daddy is because every time she sees him on television she will go to the set and say 'There's my daddy, Eddie Irvine's my daddy.' She's really proud of him and gets really excited every-time she sees him on TV. In the future, I hope they both get to know each other. She's still young now but I hope he'll be there for her when she's older. Professionally, I hope he wins the World Championship, and I hope he'll be happy.

I don't know if we will ever get back together. So many things can happen. If it is meant to be then it will happen. I believe in fate and destiny. We were in Hong Kong once and we went to the park. Eddie started to read some magazines he'd bought, but when we sat down two Indian guys suddenly appeared and came up to us. One of them said to Eddie 'You're very lucky. I've never met anyone like you but you're very lucky, you can spend your money because you'll always make more.' I thought, that's good news! But it was also very strange as usually a fortune teller will go to the woman, not the man, but he was very definite about approaching Eddie. Then he said to me 'Don't worry what he says, he's got a good heart and he's very lucky.' That was back in 1992. The fortune teller was right and I'm sure the next ten years will bring more excitement and hopefully, happy times for all of us.

My first impression of Maria was 'Wow, there's a very good looking girl. She was walking down the Pit in Macau, and I got a photograph taken with her. Three days later, I met her again in a night club. She was living in Macau, I was living in Europe, but we kept in contact, then I decided to live in Macau and commute.

I have always been attracted to mixed races, and Maria is a beautiful, intelligent girl. She is also very easy to be with, very easy to get on with, and at the same time, she's great fun. I just went along with the flow. She's a bright lady, well she must be to have gone out with me! I have to say that I enjoyed being spoiled. Even now I still think Maria is fantastic – she's great with me, brilliant with my mum and dad, and incredible with Zoe. Maria's always been a star, that's why I went out with her for so long. I was a lot more attached to Maria than any other girl before her, and I care about her a lot, so if that's love, then I love her. I care what happens to her.

It basically broke up because I'm a loose cannon. I was a loose cannon before Formula One and in Formula One. I don't know if that will ever change. I can't remember asking Maria to marry me, but that doesn't mean I didn't. I think my head has been banging about in a racing car too long. I do remember sending her an umbrella as she didn't want to come to England as the weather was bad.

I still have a relationship with Maria although it's not the same as it was before. We get on very well. The only thing we ever argue about is where she's going to live. I feel bad in a way that Maria is still in love with me, because it would be great if we could hang around together and great if she could come to my parties, but I think it would hurt her too much. I feel responsible for that, but I don't know how to resolve it at the moment. I'm still working on that problem. Hopefully time will solve it.

I have to say that Maria has done a fantastic job with Zoe. She's a great child. I saw Maria once or twice during her pregnancy, but I really started to get to know Zoe when they came to England. I didn't see a lot of Zoe when she was a baby because I'm not a natural lover of babies. I hate the mess and most of all I hate the noise. But now I think Zoe is mega. I don't know any other kids but she seems very happy, except when I steal her sweets or her dummy. I've spent more time with her this year and really enjoyed it. We've had a laugh, played on the boat and in the sea, and just generally hung out together. Zoe is normally very shy around me but we've got a lot closer in 1999. She is not a difficult child at all, she's a great kid, but loves her bed like me, and she likes to be the centre of attention. So who's that like? It's tough keeping a child amused and she's like me in that she gets bored quickly. I really enjoy being with her, just spending time with her. I hope she enjoys being with me as much.

Maria has gone back to Macau but she'll be back. I'm sure Zoe will persuade her that Macau is not a good idea. Zoe loves her boat, her plane, her jet-ski and her toys. I'd like her to live in Northern Ireland near to my parents.

They love Zoe and treat Maria like a daughter and I think that would work really well, but we'll have to see. It's not easy to persuade Maria to do something if she's not convinced it's the right thing to do. I think it is right but she has to make the final decision. I'm very glad my family have taken to Zoe, it makes things a lot easier.

As she grows up I'd like Zoe to be what I think she is, a mix between Maria and me. I think she's more like Maria in character although Maria thinks she's more like me. She is a bit bossy, but apart from that she's like her mother. From my point of view I just want to make sure that everything goes smoothly, and I'd like Maria to be happy. I'm lucky with Maria, she's a very loving person and a great mother. She does a great job bringing Zoe up.

KATHLEEN IRVINE

Zoe has given us a new lease on life. It's great to have her around, she's non-stop and she's up and at them. She already knows how to wind men round her little finger. Big Ed worked when our two were growing up, now he has more time for Zoe, and I think he's really enjoying life with his grandchild.

SONIA IRVINE

I lived with them for a couple of months in Kent, and that was great. Zoe was always very quiet as a baby, she'd just play with her toys, but Maria is very calm, and I think the fact that Zoe is a calm baby is down to Maria. It's hard work looking after a baby and I think Maria has done a fantastic job. I remember once I baby-sat for a couple of hours while Maria went out.

Zoe was changed before Maria went out, then I fed and changed her again, and got my own dinner. She managed to roll over and get my orange juice all over her, so I grabbed her like a parcel and went upstairs and changed her again. Three times in two hours, Maria couldn't believe it!

PETER FOX

I think Eddie is quite emotional and although many of his different girlfriends are just a bit of fun, when he meets someone he connects with he does fall in love. I'm sure he still loves Maria. I believe that because I saw how much he was in love with her when he lived in Macau with her. He used to call her his little 'puchy puch' and he certainly said he loved her when we were in Macau. There was real love there. He'd genuinely be worried Maria was checking out what he was doing. If we went clubbing he'd say 'I can't talk to that girl. If Maria finds out I'm a dead man.'

I've been in love like that and when the relationship finishes you don't stop loving them. The situation changes, but you don't fall out of love. Maybe you don't want to be around them anymore, but you still love them. I think Maria is the only one who really got to him and made him realise that you have to give people a bit of respect. I think he's got a lot of respect for Maria, because she's someone who would bite back. She wouldn't just go, 'Okay, Eddie, I'm sorry,' she'd just walk out and leave him saying 'You're an idiot, I don't want to know you.' At the same time, though, she was incredibly loving.

I'd like to see him end up with Maria, she's brilliant
for him and she keeps his feet on the ground and his
head together. But I'm not him, and I think whoever
he ends up with will have to wait until he's finished
racing. While he's a racing driver and so successful,
he's got all the attention and it would be hard for him
not to be tempted. I think all the models he goes out
with are just a distraction and part of the image, but
that he'll be different once it's all over and he can go
back to being a normal human being. I mean who
wouldn't be tempted by beautiful women throwing
themselves at you? We'll see, he could end up being a
bachelor for the rest of his life, or marry five times. It's
all yet to happen for him.

CHAPTER 7

Silverstone

Silverstone was a defining moment, first because Michael had his accident and broke his leg, and second because shortly after Silverstone my future was decided.

The spotlight is always on the British drivers at the British Grand Prix, and 1999 was no different. The attention remained high from the major test the previous week, and there were all sorts of stories circulating about my future. I gave a press conference for the British press at the test, and at that point I knew that I wouldn't be a Ferrari driver for 2000. I hadn't been told officially but Enrico and I had heard that a decision had been made. But I couldn't let the press know, so we played cat and mouse. One of the questions was, was I too wild to go to McLaren? I've always hated the premise behind a question like that. People actually in Formula One know that I am serious – no one gets to be one of the top drivers in Formula One if they mess around. Just because I don't go around with a serious expression on my face all the time doesn't mean I take life easily. Anyway, as I said, McLaren would take Billy Connolly if he was the fastest driver.

I did a shoot for Tommy Hilfiger on one of the test days, which is part of their European Ad Campaign, and it would have been quite a laugh, if it hadn't been so cold. I've got used to doing photoshoots and that kind of thing, it's part of my job and it earns the money. Enrico had always said that it's easy to get me to a party full of beautiful women, and very expensive to get me to a party full of businessmen. I guess that's still true.

Then it was into the weekend. Once again, the car was better than at the test. The current technical regulations make the cars very wind sensitive, so I was hoping that the good set up I found on Friday would hold for Saturday. As it turned out I qualified fourth and Michael was second. I couldn't really complain about being on the second row, as I hadn't done enough running on new tyres during the previous week's test, so it was difficult to set up the car to run properly with the new rubber. I had a lot of understeer until we solved it for my final run. I then pushed as hard as I could but the track was getting slower, so I was quite happy with the second row.

However, on race day everything changed. I made a really good start and Michael made a really bad one and so I was ahead of him. My impression was that Michael tried to out brake me and locked up the brakes; he then came off the brakes to unlock them as the car wasn't slowing down.

We hadn't been told about the red flag, there was no red flag on the Hangar straight, and so he went on the brakes again and that's when the rear nipple failed. He probably thought he'd go off and come back on again. I thought 'He ain't coming through until they radio to me to let him through.' It was not my intention to put him off, that would never have been my intention. Michael is a fair driver and so am I, we were simply racing. I braked as late as I could brake, he was off line and the track was dirty. The next thing he's locked the brakes and he's coming flying past me. I thought there is no way he's going to stop. We've seen the replay, he locked immediately on the brakes, came off the brakes to unlock the wheels, re-hit the brakes, and then they failed and he ended up off the track.

I didn't know what had happened to him until after the race. They don't hold up the race for a driver to get back to the pits and change cars, so I just thought he'd taken too long to get back. The team's objective was to concentrate on the race, and try and win it. I overshot the Pit Stop, and that cost me victory. It was the first time I'd come into the pits when the McLaren guys were already waiting for their driver. Once I had got past them, I realised how close my guys were to them, and it was pretty obvious that I wasn't going to be able to get stopped in time to get into my pit in the right position. As I'd overshot, they weren't immediately able to get the fuel hose on the nozzle.

I was surprised when Jean Todt criticised me afterwards. Michael goes into the wall in Canada and 'Oh, well, it's just one of those things.' I go two feet wrong in a pit stop and I'm castigated. Jean does a fantastic job, he has brought Ferrari back to be a team that can fight for the World Championship. He has found the right people and put them in the right places at the right time, and made sure they work to the best of their ability. But just sometimes he comes out with comments that I really disagree with.

He and Michael have formed a very close relationship which works well for them. I don't think I could have the same kind of working arrangement, I like my space almost to the point of being fanatical about it.

After Michael went into that wall at Silverstone, everything changed; or rather it did and it didn't. After that we were level on points and it was my great chance to go for the Championship. In other ways nothing changed. People thought Michael would be back after a couple of races and that he would take over again. There was still the feeling that in the meantime I was just holding things together. In

Austria before the race, Ross Brawn said to me 'What you've got to make sure of is that Hakkinen gets as few points as possible, so when Michael comes back he's still in with a chance.'

However, the team are behind me now and have been for a few races. But the question of whether Michael was coming back or not certainly confused the issue. We weren't sure which side was running with the ball, and that clouded things somewhat. The pressure is on Jean Todt in these circumstances to say what the strategy is going to be. The better I did the more difficult Jean Todt's job became. He was in a tricky situation to say the least.

On the Tuesday after the Silverstone race Enrico and I met Luca di Montezemolo and Jean Todt in Bologna and they told us they didn't want to renew my contract. It seemed strange timing to say the least considering I was their hope for the Championship! Even so, it wasn't a surprise as Enrico had known for ten days. Enrico knows everyone in motor racing and people talk. I think we might have found out even before Mr Agnelli. As I've already said, I had agreed to join Honda for 2000, but when the deal started to fall apart, I had had to look around again. Although I wasn't going to say so in the meeting, Ferrari was a dead duck for me now because I felt I was always going to play second fiddle there. Even so, we kept on talking to see if there was a way forward. We also discussed strategy and I explained about how I think there should be two pit crews, and we talked about my concerns about tactics being geared to the number one driver at Ferrari.

This can have a big effect. For example, in Austria

where I won this year, it was decisive. I probably wouldn't have won if Michael had been in the race, because of the race strategy. He would have come in one lap after me, and I would have had to come in one lap early. In that last lap I pulled two seconds over DC, which got me ahead of him and I won the race. If Michael had been in the race he would have won if he'd been in a similar position, and I'd have come third and looked like a complete tosser.

I don't know whether McLaren have a better strategy in allowing Coulthard and Hakkinen to fight it out without a number one status. Coulthard and Hakkinen aren't Michael Schumacher – Ferrari have the best driver so they put most of their eggs in one basket and normally that's the right thing to do. I do not think it's particularly sporting, and it's not particularly good for team morale, but it's good for the final result. This year, though, it's backfired as I feel I have lost points as a result which would have been useful now.

In spite of all this, Enrico and I had let Ferrari know after Monaco that I would be available for one more year. At that time there had been no immediate response, apart from the fact that Gianni Agnelli, the Fiat Boss, had called for me to stay, which was widely reported in the press. However, I clearly didn't fit in with Ferrari's future strategies. My view is that Michael was just looking after his own interests, which is the right thing to do.

Ferrari were talking to everyone as they do every year, and finally settled on Rubens Barrichello. But if Ruben's experiences are like mine, I don't think he'll feel he has equal status at Ferrari. I believe Ferrari are committed to Michael as their number one driver. That is their strategy and they have to live with it. Michael has his contract and that is it.

The budget at Ferrari is not as big as people think. There is no bottomless pit of money, so having adopted this approach, they don't have a lot left over. From a business point of view I think they've done a restrictive deal with Michael. He wanted the status of driving for Ferrari and I think he sells a lot more hats and T-shirts because he's Michael Schumacher, the best driver in the world, but also because he drives for Ferrari. For their part I feel Ferrari have locked themselves into one driver and left themselves little room for manoeuvring.

My understanding of the deal with Michael is that it is unusual because they ordinarily pay a driver what he's worth less the amount of money they think he'll make in sponsorship terms from being a Ferrari driver. If they think you're worth X and then calculate that you'll make Y, they pay you X minus Y. I've always had a lowish retainer, but then I've had the opportunity to make money from being a Ferrari driver. It isn't always the best option as, although Ferrari think they've saved some money, the driver usually ends up running around like a blue-arsed fly. Ron Dennis at McLaren has a more clinical approach. He pays you a wage and that's it, you're not allowed to do anything for anyone, end of story. McLaren expect you to concentrate on the racing which, if you consider the investment, is probably the more sensible way to go. You wouldn't really invest five million pounds in a race horse and then parade it around supermarkets for promotional work.

Since we didn't have an immediate reaction from Ferrari after Monaco as to whether they wanted me to stay for another year or not, Enrico carried on talking to various teams. On the grid at Magny Cours, Adrian Newey had come up to me and said 'Would you like to beat Michael?' The answer was obviously yes, so we started to discuss the possibility of me going to McLaren. Who wouldn't like the chance to work with Adrian Newey? I have to say that I was surprised that Newey didn't go to Ferrari when he was offered it. Everyone loves Italy when they come here. He should come to Italy at some stage, just for the experience.

I spoke to Ron Dennis and I think he was keen to have me. However, in the end we didn't get down to detailed negotiations. I think one of the major reasons Ron decided to keep DC was because he didn't want him going to another team as he didn't want his rivals to know what they were up to, and he didn't feel there was enough of an advantage in taking me to risk the change. He said he felt I was better than DC but not enough to risk taking me. He also said he owed it to DC to stick by him as he'd had such a run of bad luck.

In some ways I would have loved to have driven for McLaren, but in other ways I wouldn't. Technically, they're fantastic, but there's some other stuff that I'm not sure about. I remember when DC was asked a question at the British Grand Prix about whether he was worried about brake problems, as Ron had said that had caused Hakkinen's wheel to come off. DC just said 'It looked to me like the wheel just came off, so no I'm not worried about brake problems.' Then he quickly said 'Oh, maybe brake failure had caused the wheel to fall off.' He seemed to me to be reluctant to contradict his team boss. I was still in two minds but if it had come up I think I would have gone for it. Mind you, if things had changed at Ferrari, I wouldn't have hesitated about staying there for another few years.

My manager Enrico Zanarini has always negotiated with the teams. I have to say that Enrico and I are the best team. We are very different but we complement each other well. I am very undiplomatic, I go in and cause shit, get my point across, then he smoothes things down. There have been times when something goes wrong, and I would have walked away from a deal, but Enrico will hold on and say 'Keep calm', and then before you know it we've got another deal out of them. He's exactly the type of person I need. At the same time he needs me too. I think I'm a better businessman than him in some ways. I'm harder at the negotiating table, and I see a deal more clearly even if he's a lot better at keeping a deal actually together. We have different talents. He's a great PR man, great at keeping the sponsors sweet. My strength is in closing deals.

You couldn't find a nicer person than Enrico and we've become friends as well as business partners. Sometimes I think he's too nice, and people take advantage of him, whereas they would never take advantage of me. He's a good laugh and we party together. He loves to party. When I was living with him, I wouldn't see him that much, because he'd be arriving home at maybe eight o'clock, after work, and then he'd go out at 11.30 or midnight, and then be up at eight the next morning for work.

ENRICO

I first met Eddie in 1990 when he was driving in F3000. I was the manager of Emanuele Naspetti who, along with Eddie and Heinz Harald Frentzen, was one of three drivers for Eddie Jordan. Eddie finished third in the Championship that year, and he won at Hockenheim. It was Emanuele who said I should watch Eddie as he was very good and very strong mentally.

At first I found him a bit introverted, but funny. I was working with Jordan to get sponsors, and in 1993 Eddie came to Formula One to race with Jordan. When I got to know him, I liked him. I found him straight and easy to deal with, although I found it difficult to understand Eddie's accent at first. We are opposites: he's very impulsive and gets upset very quickly, but then gets over it very quickly. He's aggressive but I'm a bit more diplomatic. He's shy, but after you know him for a while his true feelings come through. He thinks it's weak to show emotion, so if he has a soft spot for somebody he will never show it until he gets to know you. People think he's hard, but he's not. He has a strong attitude, which has brought him success, but deep down he's a really nice guy.

We have become very good friends and we party together as well as do business, and I think that helps us to understand each other. We both know how to work hard and how to play hard. Considering that we work so closely together we have had very few problems. We've never had a fight and so far have always managed to solve any problems that might have occurred.

We always try and get involved with sponsors who already have dealings with Formula One, as they understand the sport, and the importance of being

associated with a Formula One driver. You both talk
the same language. The sponsor needs to understand
that a top sportsman has many commitments but that
he can still exploit the association to the full, whilst
working around those other commitments. A top
sportsman, and Eddie is particularly good at this, will
give 100% to whatever he is focused on at that
moment, whether he's driving or appearing at a sponsor's event. Eddie and I always work closely together
to help the sponsor get the best, and he is very good
with sponsors. He'll ring them up when he wins and
say 'Am I mega or what?' and they love that.

The trickiest aspect of my job is the press, as sometimes he can be a little too forthright and then you
spend the rest of the day putting out the fires. He
gives the impression of not caring, but when I had a
hernia operation he was on the phone more times than
my mother, so there is no doubt that he cares about the
people he's close to. If you're loyal to him, then he will
always be loyal to you.

He doesn't have too many bad habits, but he does
tend to go crazy in front of other people, and I think it
is best if you don't show your temper. He gets bored
easily and he hates attention, except when it's from
beautiful girls. He's actually great at chatting up
women. He's a clever operator and can talk shit for
hours. When I meet a girl I need to find something of
common interest, and then maybe we get together, but
he can talk to girls who have nothing to say. That's
really clever, he can talk for hours saying nothing to
girls who understand nothing.

He can get his hands on anything he wants at the moment, which is fascinating to watch from a distance. He's on a winning wave, he can score with anyone he wants to, and confidence is sky-high. At the moment he is very much in love with Anouk, so he has given up the chatting up routine, but he is a master at pulling the girls when he puts his mind to it. He also loves to do business and make money. He's pretty astute at it and I think he'll make a good businessman when he gives up racing. He's got his plane, cars, boat, houses, and even me his manager, all for less than the market value. I love my work so I'm very happy to be working with him and creating a great business base for us both.

When the Honda deal fell apart, we had to look around and also we kept talking to Ferrari. At the Spanish Grand Prix I talked to Jackie Stewart and said we'd like to be at the top of his list. Then Jackie sold the team to Ford. We didn't know that he had done this until the announcement later in the season. We also talked to Jordan, which is like a family to Eddie, but in the end the opportunity of Jaguar was too good to miss. Eddie had always wanted to be associated with a motor manufacturer and to be associated with Jaguar in Formula One is incredible. He is really look-ing forward to the challenge of leading a big team and I don't think he's sore about leaving Ferrari. He is a realist and he knows that if he had remained, he would always have been number two to Michael, and for a driver as talented and ambitious as Eddie that would be an impossible situation to take any longer.

There were other problems with the Ferrari deal. We had a performance-related contract with Ferrari, which Eddie was disappointed about. He wanted to be paid for his work, not paid on the basis of how well he did. Knowing he was going to live in Michael Schumacher's shadow, he thought it would be more difficult to earn good money from such a performance-related contract. Actually, though, he's made more money each year with Ferrari. From 1996 to 1999 he's had an increase in the performance-related side, and also an increase in wages. Ferrari might have felt his contract would be advantageous to them but in the end they have had to pay out a lot more than if he'd just had a normal basic pay deal.

When we were told on the Tuesday after Silverstone by Mr Montezemolo and Mr Todt that Ferrari had decided not to renew Eddie's contract, we weren't surprised as we'd already made an agreement with Jaguar. Ferrari had a very difficult decision to make regarding Eddie. They had a team structured round Michael Schumacher and that had to influence their decision. Mr Todt appeared to me to be the executor not the decision maker, and in my opinion he had presented two or three different scenarios to Mr Montezemolo and the board of Fiat. In the end the decision is taken by the president but has to be agreed by the board. They had a choice. They could have changed the parameters within which Michael Schumacher operated. They could have said to him Eddie is a good driver, he's fast and we want him, or alternatively they could have appeased Michael.

I think Eddie was becoming too much of a problem for the Ferrari setup. Eddie could influence the communication machine through the media and in my opinion that was perceived as negative. Also he was no longer a second rate driver. Michael has signed a contract until 2002 with money from Fiat, and Eddie's public profile was growing. Eddie is very popular both within the team, and within Italy. So in the end I think they decided it was best overall if Eddie left. That can be the only explanation. Otherwise, what sense can there be in getting rid of a driver going for the World Championship? If Eddie goes on to win the World Championship they'll have to examine their decision to get rid of him very hard.

Someone in the long run may have to pay for this ridiculous situation. Why pay $25 million for a driver? If Eddie arrives at the last race with a chance to win the title, he will have matched everything that Michael has achieved at Ferrari. After Silverstone he came out from under Michael's shadow and now I think Eddie just about has the full support of the team. For a time they thought Michael would be back and they didn't think of Eddie as a leader nor fully appreciate his qualities.

There was talk that Eddie is not aggressive enough, but he's brought the car home and has scored vital points. World Championships are not won on taking risks. Each year he's got better and what he has achieved is unique – very few other drivers have improved their standing in the World Championship year after year.

Finally, on Saturday 4 September Ferrari announced that they had signed Rubens Barrichello. Eddie was on his way to board his boat the *Anaconda*, where Sonia, his parents and his daughter, Zoe, were waiting for him. It wasn't just the end of an era just for him, but for all of us including Sonia who has worked so closely with him at Ferrari.

SONIA IRVINE

It wasn't a big surprise as we'd known for a while that they were going to sign Rubens. Even so I was disappointed about leaving Ferrari. You always think of Ferrari as the ultimate, and although there have been ups and downs, I've made a lot of good friends there. For four years I've got to know how a team works and how to achieve my objectives within that team, and now it's all back to square one. It's the end of an era. But you've got to move on. I'll go to the next team and I'll learn how they work. But even so I feel bit sad about leaving. It is not just a case of being in a glamorous job with a glamorous team – most of the time my job has just been hard work. I never think of it as being exciting. I just go in and do my tasks, the race finishes, I go home and go on to other things. So that's not the reason I'm sad.

I don't think Edmund was disappointed as he couldn't really stay as number two to Michael. Things never stay the same. He's had quite a while to prepare for this, and for him moving to Jaguar is a big challenge. He can help build the team and be a leader and he very much wants that kind of challenge. In some ways for him it's a natural step from Ferrari. There he was number two in a very big team, now he'll be the star in a team that promises to become a big fish, and with Jaguar it has real potential. For him that must be very exciting. Eddie is very strong mentally, he'll have turned the situation round in his head to get the most out of it, which is what both of us have been brought up to do.

Now he's got a great chance of winning the World Championship but if Michael was still there he wouldn't be in contention, so we have to keep it in perspective. When Ferrari released the information about Rubens signing for them we had to make our own press statement on the back of theirs, just saying that Edmund had had four good years with Ferrari, he's in contention for the World Championship, but unfortunately, he couldn't stay as number two to Michael.

I think the fans can't fail to be surprised that Ferrari have chosen not to keep a driver who's aiming for the World Championship, but its for them to explain and not for me to criticize. Within the team, there have been quite a few rumours for quite a long time. Some of the mechanics have come up to me and said 'What's wrong, why aren't they keeping Eddie?' I don't think it's because Rubens is a better driver. Eddie's driven with him before and psychologically Eddie was a lot stronger. I don't know if Rubens has developed since then. I suppose I'm biased, but I think Edmund has come on as a driver a lot in the last few years. He's matured, and he's also now very strong psychologically. It's very difficult to drive as the number two knowing that if you're leading a race and the number one driver is behind you, you'll have to move over for him. Psychologically, that's quite a big thing to deal with and he's been coping with that for four years.

EDMUND SENIOR

I think it's a good opportunity for Eddie to go to another team as the team leader. For some reason Ferrari didn't want Eddie any more. Some people say it was because Michael was Ferrari's number one driver, but I think that's a bit stupid. It should be a team thing. The way to win World Championships as Williams and McLaren have done seems to be to work as a team, not have a number one around whom the whole team revolves. Different drivers drive differently and have different preferences on set up and in testing, so it seems to me to make more sense to base the team around two equal drivers and have two major inputs.

I don't think Eddie is put out by it. He just seems to accept that one door closes and another opens. That's the way he's always been. It would be ironic if he wins the Championship now that he's not going to be at Ferrari.

ENRICO

In spite of the sadness of leaving Ferrari, we are very pleased that Eddie will drive for Jaguar next year. We have signed a three-year contract with the team that is not performance related, which will make him the third best paid driver in Formula One after Michael Schumacher and Mika Hakkinen. There are no number ones or number two positions at Jaguar, but the team's efforts will be concentrated on Eddie, and he will be the front man. Johnny Herbert will be a good team mate for Eddie; they got in a bit of a discussion in Australia some years ago, but that's all water under the bridge. Johnny was three seconds a lap quicker than Eddie in Formula Ford, but I think Eddie's going a bit better now!

We are already thinking in terms of marketing strategy and I think we have a winner. To be the first Formula One driver to drive for Jaguar and associated with Ford and Jackie Stewart is fantastic. We couldn't have hoped for a better drive.

When Ford bought Stewart and Jaguar consequently came in that made it the dream combination. There might not be so much chance of winning the World Championship with Jaguar initially, but I think that my experience at Ferrari puts me in an ideal position to lead the team. Mika Salo is a great guy to work with, but I've seen the difference between him and me in terms of experience gained in driving for a big team. He's at the stage I was at when I joined Ferrari, and it brought it home to me how much I've learnt in four years with Ferrari. It has given me great confidence to go to a new team like Jaguar and be a leader.

Driving for Jaguar also means I can live in Italy for two or three months of the year without getting all the attention of a Ferrari driver. I like a challenge and I'm really looking forward to the challenge of leading Jaguar to success in Formula One.

While all this was going on excitement was building for

the Austrian Grand Prix. The press got together and started to accuse me of shouting my mouth off, and *Autosport* came out with the headline 'The Talking Stops Here, Time for Motormouth Irvine to prove he can beat McLaren pair.' 'Motormouth' may be a bit strong. I'm outspoken, I say what I think, but in my mind there's no harm in that. The actual problem is that I speak to the Italian press, it gets translated into Italian as I speak to them in English, then it goes to German for the German press, then back to English for the English press. Often the difference between what's printed and what's said is incredible. I did an interview earlier this year and I said to the journalist 'I don't know if Michael is going to help me, but as I'm ahead of Hakkinen, it would make sense for Michael to come back and help me.' The resulting headlines are 'Schumacher, You're Finished, You've Got to Help Me Now.' To me it's comical, it's great entertainment, but Ferrari get pissed off about it. Every time I arrive at a race Jean Todt says 'Eddie, did you say this?' and quizzes me about various articles. I just say 'Jean, don't waste my life by talking about this any more.' At the end of the day, there's no point going over old news, it's always the next day's fish and chip paper anyway.

. . . .

CHAPTER 8

Racers

Wherever I go I tend to leave my mark. From Jordan to Ferrari and now to Jaguar, people form quite strong opinions about me – I suppose it is partly to do with living in something of a goldfish bowl. I also have my own views on the men I work with in the world of motor racing.

I wouldn't say I had a lot of friends in motor racing, as there's so much bullshit around, but there are a few who are very genuine, like Ian Phillips, the Commercial Director of Jordan. Ian is my best friend in motor racing, he's one of the nicest people you could meet, very straightforward and down to earth, which is a rare thing in Formula One. We've had some laughs and some good parties but he also helped me to get to know my way around the Paddock when I first came into Formula One.

It goes without saying that there are some real arseholes in Formula One. In addition, some have serious psychological problems. Formula One seems to attract such people and there are very few individuals who don't have complexes of some sort. Ross Brawn is a rare exception. He is very good as he's as hard as nails, and he can be a bastard when he has to be, but he's also very level headed. Ian is maybe a little too nice for Formula One, and sometimes he has been abused by people who used him. I don't think I have a complex about anything and I'll certainly never get used. I can be a bigger arsehole than anyone else when I have to be.

I am very cautious about people and it takes a long time before I think of someone as a friend, but I'm pretty perceptive and am usually right when I make a decision about someone. Maybe when I've left Formula One I'll be a bit more relaxed, but right now I tend to start from the assumption that everyone wants something from me, and only then will I weed out the good from the bad. At the end of the day, though, I'm happy with my little band of friends, and I do mix with some of the Formula guys like DC, Jacques and Trulli. DC is a good driver; I'd say he's not as good as Hakkinen and Michael, but he's in the next little group. I think I'd be quicker than him, and although you'd expect me to say that, I do believe it. I really don't think McLaren have maximised DC's image, he seems sanitised to me, and I don't think that in the long term that will do him any favours. In my opinion he's technically better than Mika, but Mika's more naturally talented. What's more, Mika's a little more consistent than DC, and that is important when you're counting the points.

Mika's a nice enough guy and he's quick and very talented. However, he's made a couple of mistakes that must have stuck with him. Errors he made when leading at Imola and Monza, causing him to go out of the race, must really haunt him. Next time he's in the lead he'll probably be twitchy about going on the limit, and that will make it easier for us to catch him. I think the speed advantage of the McLaren might be affected by Mika being unsettled about his own ability to bring the car home without going off the track. He could have almost got the Championship sewn up if he hadn't thrown away the twenty points. In some ways I wouldn't like to be in his position, but Mika is a top driver, and like me, he'll have the ability to turn round a negative situation and make it work for him.

I was also bemused by his reaction after Spa. You just

don't behave like that. Not celebrating with champagne was one of the most disappointing things I've seen. If you feel like that you sure as hell don't show it. I think that all that, combined with the tears after Monza, could cause him problems. After all, it's pretty useless being fast and then seemingly throwing it away. Somehow or other he has to put those mistakes a long way behind him and get on with the job in hand, but I reckon he'll manage to do it.

Some people say Damon is susceptible to stress but I don't agree with that. For sure he was lucky to get the Williams drive, but he still won the World Championship, and you don't do that without talent and determination. I have to confess at the start of the 1999 season I wondered why he was bothering and even thought that he might be in it just for the money. But if you look at races like Spa, where he did a great job to qualify where he did, you have to say he's the original comeback kid. Just when you write him off, and in fact by announcing his retirement he had written himself off, back he bounces. You need balls to go round Spa, and his performance proved he's getting back in the game again.

A lot of people say that of all the Formula One drivers, Jacques Villeneuve is the one most like me. We both speak our minds, but I think the similarity ends there. In at least one respect we are completely different. I'm not sure if he knows the value of money at all. We went into a shop once and he bought sixty CDs and didn't know any of the artists. You ask him how much his plane costs him to run and he doesn't know and doesn't care. I am totally different, I know exactly how much everything costs, and if I'm getting a good deal compared to other things. I have people working for me who save me money by always getting the best deal going, but I always know how much they're spending. I know what my toys cost, and I take an interest in them.

Jacques is showing his talent and really driving out of his socks right now but he and I don't always share the same opinions. Sure, the new regulations are not the way to go, but I wouldn't say they are a total waste of space. The cars do need to be slowed down. Jacques had said bravery is everything but potentially, I think it can lead to stupidity. At Spa this year he said 'I just had to challenge myself to go flat through Eau Rouge.' Well to me the challenge is to get from the start to the finish line as quickly as possible. Taking risks is just a very cheap thrill. But even if Jacques may have some weird opinions that I differ from at least he's an individual and I like people who stand out from the rest. Also, you can have a good laugh with Jacques which says a lot. I really like hanging out with him.

As well as drivers, other people have been pretty influential in my years with Ferrari.

JEAN TODT, TEAM BOSS, FERRARI

The first time I heard Eddie Irvine's name was in Suzuka in 1993 when he got into a fight with Ayrton Senna. He'd just got into Formula One and straight into a fight with one of the legends, so it brought him to everyone's attention. I was already with Ferrari as I joined the team as Team Boss in July 1993, and I was part of the World Council meeting when Eddie had to come and respond to everything concerning that incident.

At the end of 1995 we had to find a driver to put

next to Michael Schumacher for the 1996 season and Eddie seemed to be the one driver we could choose. One disadvantage of this was that we had to pay Jordan to get him out of his contract with them, which came to quite a significant amount. I met Eddie in Estoril, during the Portuguese Grand Prix, when he came to my hotel room and we spoke two evenings in a row.

My overriding impression of him then was that he seemed to be very determined and very strong mentally. After these meetings I convinced Ferrari that it was worth paying Jordan to get him out of his contract, and having him as part of the team. In my opinion he was very brave to accept the challenge to compete with Schumacher. In the beginning he could not do as much testing as he wanted to do, as much of it was done by Michael, so it was not easy for him. But he still showed the same determination to stick with it, and I knew that better things would happen for him. I had to make him understand that and believe in it.

The first races were quite tough because it was a new car, a new team and a new way of working. I think one of the most important factors in Eddie being able to survive that first year and find his own space in the team is his mental strength. Whatever happens to him, he always manages to put it aside and get on with the job in hand, and that is one of the most important abilities to have if you're going to do well in motor racing.

He seems very relaxed but if you know him well, he's not that relaxed at all. He likes to give out a certain playboy image, like a playboy, but he has changed. In the beginning he was very badly behaved: he'd put his feet on the table and take calls on his mobile phone during meetings. I tried to explain that this was not the way to behave, and it was not the attitude we wanted from a Ferrari driver. It took him some time before he understood that. But he is really not as relaxed as he seems, he is much more focussed, much more concentrated, and much more professional than he sometimes likes people to believe. A real playboy couldn't be in contention for the World Championship. There is more to him than some people think.

I think his biggest achievement has been being able to stand the pressure of competing with Michael and still improve himself as a driver. In fact, pressure seems to bring out the best in him – he can be switched off until the last minute, and then get in the car and put in a huge amount of effort. He has closed the gap between himself and Michael and that is really something to his credit. I think there's more to come from Eddie Irvine, but being racing driver in Formula One is a very difficult job because your success is so much linked to the car, and to the team. So at a certain point the driver cannot go past the limitations of the car however good he is, and his success also depends on the team, getting the right people in the right positions, and then getting the best from them.

Personally, I don't like calling them number one and number two drivers. I think the situation was created by itself, because most of the time Eddie was behind Michael so he had to follow. But when Michael had his accident Eddie took over very well, and he continues to do well for us. We don't know when Michael will be back, the whole thing is a big question mark. We don't know if it will be difficult for Michael to drive in the beginning, we'll just have to take each day as it comes. At the moment Eddie is a key player in Formula One. But you know how things are, Formula One moves on and I think it's the same with Eddie. As long as he's there in Formula One everyone will enjoy having him, he's someone special. But he's also very unpredictable. One day he might decide to go around the world with fifteen girls, and that will be it, he won't be interested in Formula One anymore. It may come today or tomorrow. I just hope it won't come this year!

Ross Brawn, Technical Director of Ferrari.
I'd never worked with Eddie until I came to Ferrari, but I'd seen him around. The first encounter I had with him was trying to stop a fight between him and Johnny Herbert at a party in Australia. I don't know what it was about but I do remember that Eddie got carried out of the party almost horizontal. I think that was in his real playboy days; he treats racing a lot more seriously now.

When I arrived at Ferrari I got to know him and to see the determination that lies behind the party animal. Eddie is pretty distinctive, you get the two contrasts, the playboy image which he lives up to and deserves, and then you've got the very serious racing driver who is very talented and very competitive. Some people might see that as a contradiction, but I think that the racing side is such an intense activity and there's so much pressure, that the other side of Eddie is his way of getting away from it for a few days. Michael has a family and that takes him away from motor racing, with Eddie it's the boats, planes and the girls and all that. But that doesn't detract from what he wants to do. The moment he arrives at the race track or the test track, his playing side is switched off and he concentrates on the job. That's the unusual thing about Eddie, he has these two seemingly contradictory elements but in fact, they complement each other very well. Maybe ten, fifteen or twenty years ago, none of this would even be commented on. You could turn up, race a car, go out and party on a Saturday night, turn up for the race on a Sunday, and so on. It just wasn't as competitive or serious as it is now. These days most racing drivers, with the exception of Eddie, can't play hard and still drive well.

I think a lot of people don't realise how physical it is to drive a racing car. They're going through corners at 3,4 G and braking at 5G. If you or I tried to drive a racing car we'd be totally exhausted in one or two laps. We just wouldn't be physically capable of doing it. They are some of the fittest people in the sporting world, but because they sit in a racing car people just don't imagine they have to be in shape.

The main thing I've seen with Eddie this year is how his success, his race wins, have built his confidence. As a result of this he's become a better racing driver. He's much more consistent and competitive than he has been in previous years. His biggest problem has been that he's been compared with Michael Schumacher, who most people would agree is the fastest racing driver in Formula One at the moment. Michael has incredible natural talent and I think what Eddie's trying to do is to take the attitude, 'Well, maybe I haven't got that ultimate talent Michael has, but I'm pretty close. So by applying myself in a better way I can make up for that small difference in sheer driving ability.' Eddie has really started to work on that side, and make it succeed for him. He has sorted out the set up of the car and got it working how he wants it to work, rather than copying Michael. Australia was a good example of that. He went his own way and won the race. He has also become much more serious on race preparation and understanding strategy for the race. He understands that winning a World Championship is much more than being the fastest driver.

I've seen a big change in him since I joined Ferrari in 1997. In my opinion this is his best season so far, and as he's made progress every year, there's no reason why he shouldn't continue to get better. He's got quicker, in fact I would put him among the best drivers behind Michael and at the top of that group as well, and he's now got a much more complete understanding of what he needs to be successful. His drive in Austria typified the progress he has made.

I guess that people want to see the men behind the helmet, they want to have their heroes and villains.

There's a rather sterile feel to some of the drivers, they don't do very much or say very much outside of the car. By contrast, Eddie's certainly brought a lot of colour into Formula One. But from our side it can be a bit of a nightmare because Eddie says what he thinks and sometimes we've got to clear up afterwards. He's great for the media but he puts a bit more pressure on us by being so forthright. What's more, sometimes it's not in his best interests to be so outspoken because occasionally he criticises the team, and I've always felt those sort of things have to be kept within the team itself. I may be unhappy about what he's doing from a driving point of view but I'd never dream of discussing that in the press, that's for us to keep within the team. Eddie gets an awful lot of attention, and unfortunately he gets misquoted a lot and he suffers because of it.

Within the team, Eddie can be a hero or a villain, it depends on your point of view. If you're the team press officer he could be a villain, if you're the guy who's having a party with him on Sunday night he's a hero. He goes from one to the other. To me he can be both. He can be very frustrating as he has very fixed ideas on a few things that I have to argue and fight to get him to understand. I think he probably does it on purpose. I think he challenges my decisions to make sure that I've thought about what I'm going to do. With Eddie you get both hero and villain, and large doses of both.

The story of him going from number two driver to being in contention for the World Championship is very heroic stuff, and I think he has found it different being number one in the team. Before Silverstone the attention was nearly always on Michael because he was perceived as the team leader and number one. I think that Eddie, living in the shadow of Michael, didn't realise the pressure Michael sometimes gets from the media. Now he's had to live with that responsibility, and I think he's seen a different side of what that brings.

However, Eddie's very self-motivated, he's very determined; I wouldn't say he feels pressure in the normal sense of the word. If there is pressure, it's pressure he's created himself because he wants to succeed. There's no team pressure on Eddie to win the Championship. We all know what we're here to do.

The party that Ross remembers in Australia has its own story attached. The previous year was my first year in Formula One and I'd arrived in a stretch limo, which was Tina Turner's, with an actress on one arm, and a model on the other, with a bottle of champagne. Everyone was waiting outside the club, and they thought 'What has arrived in Formula One?' I didn't know how to top that entrance.

But the following year I managed it. I left the circuit late with Piers Portman, and there was a load of traffic, so when we saw an ambulance coming along the road Piers lay down in the road and I pretended to give him mouth-to-mouth resuscitation. We thought we might get a lift. It stopped but they told us to get lost when they saw what we were doing. Next, a police car comes along, stops, sees who we are, and gives us a lift to the party.

We gave them a T-shirt, and they gave us a police hat and we arrived at the party with the lights and sirens going hell for leather. An impressive entrance for what turned out to be an unimpressive party. In the end the best bit was winding Johnny Herbert up about his season.

RORY BYRNE, CHIEF DESIGNER FERRARI

From a designer's point of view Eddie is not exactly aerodynamically suited to driving a racing car. He's quite long in the body compared to his height and we take this into consideration to give him the room he needs. Eddie's pelvis sits further forward in the car than is usual, and we had to relocate a few components that we'd planned to put under his legs so he had enough room. Also he was having a lot of problems with his back – sometimes he'd be in agony and I'm sure that affected his driving – so we had to sort it out. We worked on the seat position and I think it is better this year.

We design the car to suit the driver physically. We mock up a car before the final version is built and then check the driver is seated properly, the steering wheel is in the correct position, the pedals are in the correct position, and his head in relation to the bodywork round him is also in the correct position. If the driver changes to the spare car then we have to change the controls, the pedals and the steering wheel to take his driving position into consideration.

In terms of actual design to suit his driving style, I would say that Eddie prefers a more settled rear end. Michael can drive with a fairly loose rear end, but

Eddie hates that. If he had to choose he'd settle for understeer rather than oversteer. He hates it when the car snatches out at the back, but as far as possible our objective is to get the car balanced. You can do a lot more with a balanced car, and it is easier to set up. I know that Eddie has been happier with the car this year, and so I think we have got it right.

I'm onto the team as soon as the race is over and if there is anything I can do for them I'm back in the office on Sunday night to work on improvements. Formula One is a very competitive business and if you're not on the case the whole time then you lose out. For the last few years the Championship has gone down to the wire at the last race, and that shows you how competitive it really is. McLaren might bring out a faster car at the beginning of the year, but in the end we've been up there with them and fighting it out. Who can say which is the best philosophy? We want a fast, reliable car, and so do they. In my time in Formula One, I've won two World Championships with Michael at Benetton, and narrowly lost two at Ferrari, so I reckon this is the year it should come our way again!

Luca Baldisserri, Race Engineer for Eddie Irvine since 1996.
You don't go into this sport if you can't take pressure. I've been with Ferrari for ten years and I've got used to pressure; in fact I find it exciting and that it makes me more on the ball. I couldn't do a routine job that's the same every day. Fighting for the World Championship is something that a race engineer dreams about all

his life. Now we have this opportunity to go for it.

In the first year we worked together, it wasn't easy. Eddie came from an English team and he did not believe that we Italians could do the same job. We had a bad moment at Monaco when he had spun and undone his seat straps. After the race he came in pointing to his straps and we misunderstood and changed the nose on the car. That was not too good.

When I knew that Eddie was going to be our driver in 1996, I watched some of his previous races, as I had really only taken notice of him regarding the Ayrton Senna incident and the accident he had in Brazil. Those were two bad moments for him in his career, but now I wanted to see his driving style and see how he was as a driver. We both had things to learn when he came to Ferrari and I think we have picked up a lot, and work well together now. After that first season we sat down and talked and decided to carry on together. I think we sorted out a lot of things during those discussions. At the end of the day we're working for Ferrari and we have to work for the good of the team. That said, I'm firmly on Eddie's side of the table.

There's not such a gap between Michael and Eddie now as the car has improved so much. It's a lot faster and much easier to drive. I think both drivers have good points. Eddie is quite quick in qualifying and can get everything from the car. It wasn't always like that. In the beginning he said he couldn't wring the neck of the car, by which he meant get the maximum from it, but that has changed this year, where on average he's only been about 0.28 of a second off Michael. Eddie has succeeded in changing his driving style a lot and has picked things up from Michael. The car has improved but so has the way he drives. He's worked on attacking a corner, and on finding the braking point. From Michael he's learnt that sometimes it is better to brake ten metres early and to get a much higher speed into the corner. After Michael's accident I have a feeling Eddie has missed him as a reference point, particularly in qualifying.

Whatever rubbish people might say, Eddie is deadly serious. You don't joke about winning the World Championship, and there's no doubt he wants to win it. We all want him to triumph; after all, if he takes the World Championship, then Ferrari wins it, too, so there's no doubt that we are all behind Eddie in his charge for the title.

STEFANO DOMENICALI, TEAM MANAGER FERRARI

I met Eddie when he joined Ferrari four years ago. We are basically the same age and I think this is a positive point as we have similar interests. My first impressions of him were that he was a funny guy, a little bit crazy. I like his spirit and the positive way he works, and his involvement with the guys. It is very important, especially working for an Italian team, that you spend time getting to know your mechanics and engineers, and develop a good rapport with them. Eddie's certainly done this with his guys.

The most challenging aspect of dealing with Eddie was to get him to realise the importance of doing other things apart from driving the car. We prepare a programme for every race, and in the beginning it was difficult to get him to keep to it. Soon, though, he realised what working for Ferrari meant and was very co-operative.

There are always a lot of ups and downs in Formula One, and the last few races up to Nurburgring were full of difficulties. We're doing our best to keep motivated and keep going to the end. We have to ensure everything is under control, and be calm and use our brains. In this respect we need to be as least Italian as possible! We must just keep moving ahead to win the World Championship, which we'll keep chasing and chasing.

This is an extraordinary year. Next year Eddie will be part of a new team, and we'll take lots of good memories of his time with us. I hope, though, that the best memory is still to come, and will be the ultimate prize for him and for us.

EDDIE JORDAN, TEAM OWNER OF JORDAN

My main claim to fame is that I find these urchins, by which I mean guys with talent but no money, who are looking for a home to display their talents and become World Champions, take them under my wing, and start their careers. Eddie Irvine was one of those people. I knew his father as I used to race with him in Northern Ireland in Kirkistown. But the young Eddie Irvine was a nightmare. He drove for Crossle, they sacked him, he drove for Murray Taylor, they sacked him. But in my infinite wisdom I got him into F3000. He then disappeared to F3000 in Japan and I think that was the breakthrough for him. He was at home out there, there were a lot of models and good looking girls, and he knows how to party as well as deliver on the track.

He then came back to me before going onto Ferrari and now he has made his name and his fortune. I think now he is right to leave Ferrari, taking into consideration the fact he was understudy to Michael Schumacher. He had no alternative. He now has the challenge of going to a great team like Jaguar, who will have a great future and I think he has more than proved he has the potential to be a team leader and handle pressure and work to develop and shape a team.

The question around the Paddock is which Eddie is the richest, Irvine or Jordan? I have to say that Ferrari helped Jordan to survive. They paid us something like four to five million dollars to buy him out of his contract with us. After signing we were sitting by Lake Lausanne feeding the ducks and we rang Bernie Ecclestone and I said 'Bernie, we've just had a major result, I've just tucked up Ferrari for yet another four mill.' Irvine was happy because he had got a three-year contract, and we were happy because it meant survival for Jordan.

The man who really believed in Eddie Irvine was James Hunt. He was one of the Marlboro consultants finding young talent, and he said that both Mika Hakkinen and Eddie Irvine would make it big time, and he was absolutely right.

However, I have to say that Eddie Irvine is not the kind of guy you'd want your daughter getting involved with. Last year I was shocked when I discovered that my daughter had bumped into this vaguely familiar-looking guy while jetskiing, who had started the chat up line on her. She came back and said she fancied this guy and was going to have drink on his boat. I was delighted, until I discovered it was Eddie Irvine. Then I just couldn't cope, I mean Eddie Irvine with your daughter, it is suicidal for any father to even think about. I was over there like a shot. The last person I want any of my daughters to have anything to do with is Eddie Irvine. Great driver, great guy, but just stay away from my daughters!

He's outspoken and loud mouthed, but that is very much the character of today's Irishness. Being Irish is now quite fashionable and he's part of the new breed that's coming up and taking over the world.

IAN PHILLIPS COMMERCIAL DIRECTOR OF JORDAN.

Eddie would be the best World Champion that Formula One has had since James Hunt. We need a glamour boy, a young single guy who knows about living life to the full. He's great company, full of life and personality, and I've had some great times with him. I really enjoy his company, he can lift a party and make it go with a bang. He knows how to work hard, and he knows how to play hard, and he's my kind of person. I think he is really the personification of Formula One and all it stands for – the glamour and the grit are there in equal amounts. In an era where there aren't many true personalities, he has bridged that gap between sport and celebrity. He can capture both the news and the sports pages and there aren't that many sports stars who can do that. He really captures the imagination.

I think he was right to go to Ferrari, they've been good for him, and he's been good for them. I don't think Ferrari realise how much they'll miss him until he's gone. There's currently not another man in the Paddock who can do the job he's done for the last four years, but it's the right thing for him to leave. He needs to go on to new pastures, and feel the challenge of being the focal point of the team.

JACKIE STEWART

I remember Eddie in F3000, but not in F3. At that point he wasn't the personality he is today. I saw him when he won the support race at the German Grand Prix in Hockenheim and he wasn't smiling on the podium. I remember wishing he'd smile a bit more.

Over they years he's developed very well, and has grown in confidence and charisma. I think he has really come of age during 1999. Winning in Australia broke through the invisible wall that faces drivers who have never won a race. From that victory Eddie seemed to get a new lease on life and a whole new confidence about himself. Now he's come out of the shadow of Michael Schumacher really well. Before Michael's accident at Silverstone, I think that Eddie was as fast, and in some cases faster in 1999, than Schumacher. Schumacher was going through a poor run and Eddie was going through a good one. It must have troubled Schumacher considerably that Eddie was as fast if not faster on quite a few occasions.

It was this sort of form, combined with his maturity and confidence, that was so attractive to us. We needed a driver who we thought could win, and I think Eddie can. Right now there's something of large pile of mediocrity out there amongst the drivers. There's not enough strong talent, but Eddie is one of the drivers who has the ability to do the job. This decided, we started talking to his manager Enrico Zanarini, who looks after him very well, and then we all got together, came to my house and had a good conversation. We had several more talks along the way, including at one point a conversation at Silverstone with Neil Webster and Richard Parry-Jones, both very senior people at Ford, along with Paul, Gary Anderson and myself. Eddie was very clear about what he wanted and what he thought he was worth. At the same time he was very enthusiastic about coming to the team. I'm sure he saw the potential of the team as by that stage Ford had bought it and were obviously going to invest heavily in it and wanted to win. Eddie wanted to lead a team, and he knew that the Ford stable could provide the necessary technology, investment and money. Our business plan was to be competitive in four or five years, and Eddie will start in year four and continue through five and six, so he's in a very good position to be on the podium and to win races for us. I know he's got the ability to do it, and we really look forward to the working relationship that we're going to have with him.

I've been around the sport for a long time, but I still have a great passion for it. I like to see people doing a really professional job, and I think Eddie can do that. He's a highly intelligent man. He enjoys life, he enjoys investing, he enjoys earning money out of his own enterprise, and I like that in a man. Not enough sportsmen are like that. I think he's got the flair, the passion and the hunger to win. All those ingredients are essential if you're going to make a top job of it.

In addition, Eddie's come a long way in terms of knowing when to be respectful and what to say. In my opinion you have to toe the line when you're being paid to do a job. Eddie's going to be driving for Jaguar, which is not a casual team. It's quite a formal because it's new and they're doing this for the first time. They've never been in Formula One before, and they're jealously protecting their image. There will be things like dress codes that may not be ideal for Eddie, but he's getting paid well to do the job. He has the intelligence to know that he'll have to buckle down on those occasions. At the end of the day you have to deliver whether it's on the track or off it. Nowadays, a modern grand prix driver is as much a commercial tool being used for marketing as he is a racing driver. There's much more to being part of a team than just racing a car. I'm sure Eddie's going to be conscientious about everything.

Rubens Barrichello

I first met Eddie in Suzuka when he was just a boy. My first impression of him was that he was confident, and that he could do a very good job. I think he has probably changed as a driver – when I knew him he braked late and never worried about what was going to happen next. He's quite cool, he doesn't calculate things, it just comes.

I think I have to take the blame for the problems I had with him when we drove together. He was cold and he didn't care what was going on with other things inside the team, and that made me mad. I was always thinking of the good of the team and he was doing his own thing, so I'd have problems with the engine and he wouldn't. But that is something I blame myself for. He's not difficult to deal with, just different.

Eddie and I haven't talked about next year, with him coming here and me going to Ferrari. I think I've made the right choice; it could be my chance. I'm ambitious and I am not concerned about the pressure at Ferrari. I don't see that it will be any greater than the pressure I've had this year. I've read that Eddie's said that if I want to create my own space at Ferrari I should go as fast as possible straightaway, but we'll see how it goes. Even so, Eddie has been my best teacher as to how to deal with Michael Schumacher. He has handled Schumacher well and I like his approach of just getting on with doing your job. Eddie has great mental strength, and I hope I have learnt from him. Ultimately, it's up to me to do the job.

CHAPTER 9

Austria

People have asked me what it is like to be number one at Ferrari, seeming to presume there was some kind of religious ceremony whereby I was blessed and declared 'Number One, in the absence of the Great One.' Well, it wasn't like that at all. A lot of people at Ferrari still expected Michael to come back and take over the mantle to fight for the Championship. I've already mentioned Ross Brawn's comment about holding off Mika Hakkinen. But I think I went on to prove that I could take pressure along with the best of them. I was determined now that everyone was going to take my title challenge seriously.

For the Austria race I was third on the grid, with a gap of a second between me and Pole man Mika Hakkinen. The reason for this was that my brakes were inconsistent. One lap I would lock up the fronts and the next lap it would be the rears. Because of this problem I couldn't commit to the corners. From the sector times the gap wasn't so big, and I knew there wouldn't be this problem in the race. I can say I was fairly confident. My main aim was to get past David and then chase Mika. Little did I know that DC would give me a big helping hand. The A1 circuit is fun to drive so I was feeling pretty good about things. I got a reasonable start, and when DC nudged Mika off at the second corner it was the best present he could have given me. He just clipped Hakkinen's right rear wheel, making the McLaren spin, although he did manage to keep going.

But it was our pit top strategy that won the day. Coulthard and Barrichello pitted early before me and I got a fast five laps in with a light car, building up a sufficient lead before coming in. After this sprint I also required less fuel to finish the race, so could carry a lighter load, giving me another advantage. After rejoining in front of DC, I put in another few blistering laps to build up a four second lead. In the closing stages I got a bit held up with back markers, which brought down the gap between me and DC from four seconds to two. I had understeer on my second set of tyres, which got better after a while, but problems with the brakes persisted and I had to ease off. Then, right at the end, DC was catching me up so quickly I had to forget the brakes and just push for the flag.

I'd known that we weren't a second off the pace as qualifying had suggested on the Saturday. I thought it was more like half a second, and we usually go better in the actual race. People say they saw smoke coming from the car towards the end of the race; I think it must have been coming from my brain, as I was thinking of so many things.

A lot has been said about the fact that Jean Todt didn't come up to the podium, but as usual it was the press barking up the wrong tree. The team had decided to rotate people on the podium, as McLaren do. It had been pointed out to us that Adrian Newey had been on the podium, not just Ron Dennis, so Jean Todt decided it would be fair to let other senior team members have their moment of glory. It is a bit special to be on the podium, looking down on everyone, seeing all the flags and banners, and with the national anthems playing. For my victory here in Austria, Ross Brawn came up, and as he is the master strategist, I think it was right he was with me. He is a major advantage for our side. The other good thing to come out of Austria was the fact that the two McLarens had been rattled by the first lap incident. Hakkinen was not a happy bunny, and felt DC had cost him victory, but who can say? Certainly it wasn't too bright for both cars to bounce off each other, but that is what happens when two drivers in the same team are going for victory. It certainly makes for a better spectator sport, and in that respect I have to say I admire Ron for his decision to encourage both his drivers to fight for the title.

Needless to say, I went off and partied with my friends, or rather tried to party. I went to London, which wasn't a good decision as the place closes down at 10.30 pm. We ended up eating at a Chinese restaurant, and as it had to adhere to the licensing rules, we couldn't even have a beer. That's the last time I go to London after a victory. A dry night! Can you imagine Irvine and his friends doing that after a victory?

I like to enjoy life with my friends and an alcohol-free night wasn't quite what we had in mind. A lot of people think I have a load of rock stars as friends, but that's not true. I have some famous friends, but most of my mates are just normal down-to-earth guys. I do think, though, that we racing drivers have more fun than rock stars. We have the money and we don't get involved in the sleazier stuff like drugs. I fly high enough after one beer, I don't need any other shit.

I probably have four really close friends and twenty I hang around with. I know Chris Rea, Chris de Burgh and I hang around with Lisa Stansfield. Mick Hucknall is a good laugh, but most of the time I'm just enjoying drinking with my normal mates. Some of them are rich and some haven't any money at all. The ones that are rich pay for the ones that are poor. It's a bit of a Robin Hood-type situation, except we don't have to rob the rich to pay for the poor.

There's not point in me having a boat but sitting on it by myself. If we go out to dinner and then to a nightclub a bottle of vodka might be £150. Well, we buy the bottle and everyone drinks from it. There's no point in having money if you don't want to spend it. Money is important to me and I love the business side, making profits and wheeling and dealing, but I do know how to enjoy it. I have the toys – I'm the most toyed-out driver in Formula One. If I have any regrets it's that I didn't spend more money sooner. In this game, you're always worried it could all stop tomorrow, so that makes you a bit more cautious. As it's turned out, I've got more money than I need so I could have spent more. Even now, I probably don't spend more than ten per cent of what I earn, so I'm still saving about ninety per cent.

I think if I hadn't have gone into Formula One then I would have stayed in Northern Ireland and taken over my dad's business. It was a scrap-yard and I think we could have built it up to be something good. After my 'O' levels I didn't fancy going back to school and I wanted to work for my dad, but he told me to go and get a job. I got work but didn't like it, so I went and signed on. They certainly laughed at me down at the Social Security, someone who wanted to sign on for work, but didn't want any money. But it was the way I'd been brought up – Dad taught me that you didn't get money for doing nothing. After that Dad gave me a job in the scrap-yard. I didn't get any wages, what I would have got paid went towards paying for my racing. I worked seven days a week and, even though my heart was set on racing, I did enjoy the business.

People say I'm an astute businessman and I've got the Midas touch, but I don't know whether it's that or just sheer luck. My first house was a little gem in Swanley, which I bought and sold in two years doubling my money, right at the top of the property boom. Before that I made money buying and selling cars. My first serious money was when I bought a Fiesta in Northern Ireland for £700 and sold it on for £1,400.

I play with the stock market, just dabbling and moving in and out, but I haven't lost money yet. I love finance. In fact, I paid for the boat from my investment in the stock market. The only time I've ever lost money on the stock market was when I gave some money to someone else to look after. I gave them $250,000 and they lost $15,000. I went in at the right time, came out at the right time, and they still managed to lose money, so they were obviously buying and selling the wrong shares. That was the last time I let someone else invest for me. The number of guys who actually beat the market is very small. Warren Buffett is one who has made a fortune from the market. He was number four on the *Sunday Times* world's richest fifty, and is worth over £18 billion, but he lives and breathes the markets, and I wouldn't want to be like that.

But I do realise a poor investment when I see one, and as I've said, I don't feel Ferrari have made a great investment in putting all their eggs in one basket with Michael Schumacher. In Austria certain members of the team still thought he was going to come back, and as they'd invested so much money in him, it was embarrassing that I was proving so popular in Italy. To be honest, I think there was a faction within the team that were not as supportive as they could have been, but that was only a temporary thing. Gianni Agnelli and Luca di Montezemolo, men I admire and respect, want to win the Championship and I don't think they care whether it's Michael Schumacher or a monkey as long as Ferrari win it. Certainly I was winning support in the Italian press. There have always been people who supported me and people who haven't. Sometimes I feel like a football in between the two camps. At times your supporters are winning and at times the other side are winning, and into the mix you have to take into consideration the fact that the supporters can change sides from week to week. Right then I was hoping to silence my critics and make my mark again in Germany.

So onto Hockenheim and the heart of Mercedes, where McLaren always like to perform well. But I was about to spoil their party. Ferrari usually have a slight disadvantage against McLaren at the high speed circuits, and it seemed as if this weekend wouldn't be any different. I arrived at Hockenheim just two points adrift of Hakkinen. What we needed was to start going faster and outpacing the McLarens. To do this we needed to take the car forward another step that we had been working on. In the four years I've been at Ferrari we have never stood still and I think this year everyone can see the difference and that progress is definitely being made.

We were quick on Friday, but of course the time doesn't mean much. I was having trouble controlling the back end of the car and spun in the morning. I hate oversteer and a twitchy rear end, and that was something we had to work on to get right. We had new wings which made the car very fast to drive down the straights, but hard to control in the slow sections.

The good thing was that the pressure had eased a lot going to Hockenheim. The win in Austria shut the moaners up, and proved that pressure wasn't going to get to me. I think I am tough in the head, and you need to be in this game. But this time qualifying did not go all that well. Mika Salo ended up on the second row in fourth place, and I was in fifth. To be honest, I was happier with fifth than I would have been with fourth as the outside of the track is a big advantage here. There were reasons for the poor qualifying. In the middle of the qualifying session we went the wrong way with a set up change, and there was no time to change it back again for my last two runs. In addition to this, I had a lot of traffic on my final run, which obviously did me no favours.

I was thinking at this point that we should have a good look at our qualifying performances in general. We don't seem to get the best out of the car in qualifying and that was something we needed to address urgently. Once again, as in Austria, the brake balance wasn't perfect. We knew we wouldn't have that problem in race trim, but we just need to cure it in qualifying and practice.

I was fairly confident that if I could away well then I could catch the front two very quickly, and the rest would depend on strategy. But I didn't get a brilliant start and after the first lap I was boxed in and sixth. I also had a problem with my oil temperature, so I was changing gear early to use less revs and moving out of the slipstream to keep the engine cool. I decided to look after my tyres and push hard before the pit stop. Happily as things settled down I managed to get up into third when Frentzen stopped for his pit stop. DC's ten second penalty and his need to return to the pits for a splash and dash fill up, effectively ended his challenge to us. In fact it all went wrong for the McLarens, in spite of the fact that Hakkinen was the quickest driver all weekend. He got away ahead of the rest of the pack, but his pit stop let him down when the refuelling rig failed to perform, and then a blown tyre finished his race

Mika Salo was the boy wonder of the day. He was charging around leading before he got the 'call' and let me through. I knew how he felt, having been on the receiving end of that a few times. But with Mika right on the pace, we could also think of the Constructors' Championship. We came away from Hockenheim leading it by sixteen points. An eight point lead in the Drivers' Championship over Hakkinen was just what I needed. Two consecutive wins gave us a lot of confidence, although if we'd been able to look into the future, we would have known that we needed to enjoy it while it lasted. But for the moment there was much to celebrate. After Michael's accident heads had been down at Ferrari, now there was every reason to believe that we were on the way up.

My girlfriend Anouk was at the race, and it was the first time she'd seen me win, as we hadn't met before Australia, and she hadn't been around for the Austrian Grand Prix. The only other grand prix she'd been to had been Silverstone when the things that were happening round Michael's accident put a lot of tension into the race and the day, so it was good for her to see Ferrari come in one-two. She quite likes racing, although I'm not crazy about having girls at the track. But Anouk does her own thing, and that makes it easier at races.

Part of the problem is that I'm never around to actually see her. The race weekend consists of an endless round of meetings, briefings and debriefing, discussions about what we've done, what we're about to do and why. I get pissed off when the chats go on and on, which is the disadvantage of the Italians – they are the world's biggest time wasters. I like to just get on with it. Before the technical meeting on the Thursday we have a meeting with Jean Todt to decide what we're going to say to the press. In the beginning I used to feel like I was going before the headmaster, now I don't. Then we have the technical meeting to go through all the things we did for the last race, decide what we're going to do on set up, types of tyres and so on. This meeting is attended by Ross Brawn, the two drivers, Jean Todt, and the race engineers.

We have more meetings after the first hour's practice on Friday on how it went and what we'll do for the next hour. After the second hour's practice we have another meeting on what's happened and why, and the implications for our plans for the car for the weekend. Later on in the afternoon we have another meeting on what we're going to do on Saturday during practice and qualifying, including tyre choice. We then also have a meeting on the weather and spend a few hours deciding if we can change it or not!

On Saturday morning we have a meeting about what we've changed from the night before. Then we're out for 45 minutes' practice. After this we have a meeting and de-brief. Then we have another 45 minutes and after that another meeting and de-brief. Then we decide what we're going to change for the race and we'll decide on qualifying – when to go out, for how long and technical specs. Next it's qualifying and another de-brief. At 6 pm on the Saturday we have a meeting on set up. Then at 8 pm on the Saturday we have a meeting on strategy.

On Sunday we discuss what we're going to do during warm up and what we've changed from the night before. After warm up we have another meeting on how that went. Then there's the drivers' briefing. During this we talk about the circuit, what happens if we miss the chicane, penalties and things like that. After that we'll have another meeting on what we will do in the race in terms of strategy. Then there's another meeting on the rules of the race, and another meeting after the race. That's a lot of meetings isn't it?

That doesn't include the press conferences. There's now a press conference on the Thursday afternoon, one on the Friday afternoon, and then there's the post-qualifying press conference and the post-race press conference. By the end of that lot I'm pretty well talked out. Some of the press guys are good, but some aren't and I do get irritated with some of the inane questions. Generally, no one will ask anything interesting as they want to hold that back for their one-to-one exclusives rather than share it with the whole international press pack. Instead we just get the usual blather, asking about how we feel to be on pole position, the chances for the race, circuit conditions, and the likely outcome of the Championship. I thought Bernie's reply to Martin Brundle on this subject was brilliant. When Martin asked him the inevitable 'Who's going to win the Championship?' he just said, as quick as a flash, 'The guy with the most points.' A man after my own heart who doesn't like bullshit.

At that moment my points were looking good and I was confident for the next race. I like the tight, twisty circuit at the Hungaroring and on the way to Hungary I thought we'd be near the McLarens in terms of performance. In fact, I thought we probably had the edge going into this race. They'd undoubtedly helped us out in the last two meetings, but I also believe you create your own luck, and we were now higher on confidence than the McLarens, and confidence is very important in motor racing. A split second of hesitation makes all the difference between winning and losing.

The car was good from the start on the Friday and I was confident we'd developed the car in the right direction. Although the Friday's positions don't mean much, it was still good to be ahead of our main rivals. It allowed us to look forward to the rest of the weekend with optimism. As it turned out, I missed pole position by one tenth of a second, which was very disappointing as I thought that if I could get pole anywhere it would be here. All the same it was good to be on the front row, even if it meant being on the wrong side of the track, the dirty side. I knew that the start would be everything.

But Hakkinen got the best start and I was laying second. My start had been as good as it should have been on that side of the track, but after two or three laps my tyres started to go off badly, making handling very difficult, and I was having problems with the front and rear of the car, which was jumping all over the road. It was unusual for us not to get it right in the race. Before the second stop I'd been cautious but I pushed hard on the 'in' lap as I was preparing to pit, and so I was able to get out before DC. But I was struggling.

During lap 63 I lost control of the rear and ran wide at Turn 5 and then got slower and slower as the tyres got worse. Although I was disappointed to finish third, I think in the circumstances I was lucky to do that well. The important things was that we left Hungary still leading both the Constructors' and Drivers' Championships. I had a two point lead over Hakkinen in the Drivers' Championship and Ferrari had a four point lead over McLaren in the Constructors'.

I knew the next couple of races were going to be tough as we had a new aerodynamic package for Nurburgring. There would be criticism of me for not leading the team and taking charge of development, but I don't understand why everyone thought we'd go well at Spa and Monza. The development of a car goes in cycles through the year. You bolt on a new piece and it goes well; then there is a phase when there are no new parts for the races as we are testing them; then you get another step forward and so it goes on. It's the same in every team, you just don't have new parts for every race. As for leading the team in terms of development, I think that is silly. Ross Brawn is the Technical Director and Rory Byrne the Designer. Most of the aerodynamic development takes place in the wind tunnel, so short of standing in the wind tunnel and watching it, I don't see what I can do. When I have something to do I always do it, and give it one hundred per cent, but there is a limit to what driver can do on the actual technical development. We can't draw new pieces or oversee new engine development. What we do is give our input into how the car feels and the areas that are strong and weak. The technicians then go to work and develop something, and then we come back and test it.

Spa was not a happy weekend. On the Friday we realised we had our work cut out if we were to get anywhere. The handling was all over the place. I had oversteer and understeer and I was locking the front and rear brakes. I concentrated on working on set up for the race, but to be honest I made very little progress and I think the car was actually worse at the end of the session than at the beginning. At the end I tried new tyres, but I didn't push too hard as I wanted to save them for Saturday and qualifying.

Not helping matters was the speculation about Michael's return and I think the team took its eye off the ball a bit concerning this. Whether he returned or not was not the main issue. I was going for the World Championship, and that was the only thing that mattered. Michael will now have his chance next year, but for 1999, it was all over for him, and yet I think Ferrari put too much effort into his tests and whether he'd return or not.

Qualifying was disappointing. Not only were we one and a half seconds off pole, but both Jordan and Williams slipped between us and McLaren. The car felt better than on the Friday, although I had some understeer on my last run. I felt I could have gone quicker but I was slowed down because of traffic. Strategy is always important and my target for this race was to get on the podium. I didn't think it would be impossible to get past the Williams and then challenge Damon Hill, and there was always the possibility of the McLarens helping us out again.

In fact, they did kindly give us a helping hand. First of all they managed to have a bump again. DC made a better start than Hakkinen and defended his line, and then opened up again when he realised that they would both be out of the race if he kept to his line. DC winning the race was a great help to us. My fourth place gave me three useful points, and considering Hakkinen got six for second rather than ten for a win, it meant I was only a point behind him going into Monza, which was a better situation than I had anticipated. Thanks to a good start and a great strategy we managed to keep Ralf behind us, which didn't please Williams, who accused us of blocking tactics, but that's part of motor racing. We weren't doing anything illegal, or anything to bring the sport into disrepute. We were protecting our advantage, which is what we were supposed to do. After all, this is supposed to be a team sport.

After Spa the Ferrari Chairman Luca di Montezemolo took aside the technical team and told them what he thought of the situation, so I was confident that Monza would be better. There is no doubt that Ross has brought organisation to the team, as before we were trying to do everything at once and, at times, failing to achieve anything. Now everyone is in the right position and Giorgio Ascanelli is doing a great job running the factory. Giorgio is very good at what he does, he is a very experienced engineer and he makes sure the right things get done to the right standard. He oversees the operation back at base, and that helps us during race weekend, when we may need input from the factory.

It was also established that Michael would not be

returning before the races in the Far East and I think that clarified things and brought calm to the team. It was too unsettling not know about whether he would return or not – and particularly difficult for Mika Salo. So, all in all, in theory Monza should have been better. It was just as well I couldn't see into the future and discover what was going to happen to the team in the next couple of races.

CHAPTER 10

Girls, Girls, Girls

I've had so many women that I suppose you have to consider them an important part of my life. But I am very, very independent. In fact, I'm the most independent person I know. Sonia and I were brought up as kids to be independent so we'd just go off and do our own thing. I've never relied on a woman and probably never will. I've enjoyed their company and continue to love the company of women. I have made great friends with the women I've been out with, but I just don't see myself settling down to marriage and commitment.

It is easy for a guy in my position to become addicted to girls. There's nothing like seeing a new girl, and having the chase. My present girlfriend, Anouk, is an amazing looking girl, and has a great personality, so I've been a good boy for the last six months since we've been together, but before that it seemed that everything I surveyed I had to conquer. But in the end it's not that satisfying and you feel you're just chasing your tail. In that situation you can be with the most beautiful girl in the world, and the one across the table will always look better. Then you get her, and the one on the next table looks even better. But where does it all end? Usually in tears!

I do try and make it pretty clear what my intentions are, and they're certainly not honourable. I've always said I don't want to get married so the girls know that isn't on the agenda. But women are great at hearing what they want to hear and at thinking they can change you, but there's not much chance of changing my mind on this one, at least not while I'm in motor racing. It's the kind of sport where a wife and a family can make you lose your edge, cut a few tenths of a second off your time. You need to be fully concentrated on going as fast as possible, without any doubts or niggling thoughts on danger or having to stay at home and baby-sit. It's just how my life is at the moment, it doesn't mean it will always be like that.

Anouk, my present girlfriend, is a good opposite to me. She's quite serious and I'm very unserious. She's a tall, blonde, Dutch model with brains and balls. I met her in Milan. A good friend of mine, Una, who is an American model, is a close friend of hers, and one day Una rang me to say she wanted to come to Milan and have a party, and asked if she could bring a friend. I was heading for Milan that weekend so I organised a party with my mates Marcus, Ciro and Max. To be honest, I was busy as I'd pulled another girl in a bar and I was chatting her up, but I spotted Anouk as soon as she walked in. Unfortunately right then I was acting the prat and just going from one girl to the next. Needless to say, she wasn't impressed. But then things got off to a dodgy start, as she hadn't a clue who I was anyway and had been expecting a very different Eddie. Apparently, Una had said to Anouk 'I've got a friend in Milan. Why don't we go and spend the weekend with him? He's called Eddie, he's in Formula One and he's a lot of fun. We can go and stay with him.' Una then went on to say 'You'll really like him, you two will get on really well, you're quite similar in many ways.'

Anyway, Anouk works for Next in London and New York, and she was in London watching a TV programme. Damon Hill's retirement has just been announced and Eddie Jordan came on TV. Here's an Irish guy, working in Formula One. She panics and phones Una. 'Una, you told me this guy Eddie was thirty years old. Jesus what are you thinking of?'

Una was completely baffled until Anouk protested that there was no way she was going to spend the weekend in Milan with Eddie Jordan and said that maybe they should forget about it and she'd fly home to Holland to see her family and friends. Una then explained that Eddie Jordan and Eddie Irvine were both Irish and both in Formula One, but very different guys!

We had a giggle about that one and she and Una stayed, but after my behaviour at the party, Anouk woke up the next morning and realising where she was, (in my flat, but not in my bed!) she got dressed and dashed out of the flat. Anyway, later on she came down to the boat as a group of us were partying in Portofino. A friend of mine was trying with Anouk, trying and trying and getting nowhere. So I said I'd try and so I did, for a very long time.

She went back to New York and I rang her constantly. She was interested but women just play games all the time. I was pretty confident that I'd get her sooner or later, and I did work very hard for it. I always thought I was just off base camp waiting for the clouds to clear, and eventually they did. We've been going out for about six months and I've been good for six months, which is practically a record. Our relationship is very cool, and there aren't any problems. She's very independent, does her own thing, and doesn't bother me – which is how I like it. I cannot bear clingy. I really like being with Anouk, I'm just not great at expressing my feelings. Basically, being with her is brilliant.

However, I'm still at the point of trying to get her round to my way of doing things. She hates it when me and my mates talk about women and sex, but I'm helping her through it. Like all beautiful women she's been spoiled and needs to realise that if she comes out with me and my mates we're going to talk about blokey things, like we always have done.

Sometimes the language thing can be a bit of a problem. She doesn't understand me a lot of the time, which is probably why we get on so well – she hasn't worked out what I'm really like! Her English is American English and the Irish accent is very different to that. The way we say things makes all the difference, and sometimes she misses the point, which can be very funny.

Misunderstandings aren't limited to language, the press has had its bit of getting the story completely wrong. There was one story which had me leaving a qualifying session – I think it was in Austria – then flying to the airport, getting in the jet, flying to Greece, and then getting a helicopter to her hotel. Supposedly I stayed there for one hour, during which time we went through the *Karma Sutra*, then I flew all the way back to the circuit to carry on with the race weekend. Where do they get all that from? It is just so unreal. In fact, I did go to Greece, but not like that. I finished the race at Silverstone and had a bit of a party in Oxford. Anouk was working in Greece, and I was thinking of sending the boat there. So I flew with Anouk down to Greece, to spend a day there to check it out to see if it was worth sending the boat over. I was flying around in my free time, not going up and down during race weekend. It would be absolutely impossible to leave the circuit and do that kind of trip, we have too much on during race weekend.

There was another story that I went to buy a new

Mercedes with a bag of used five pound notes. What do these guys do? Does a journalist wake up one morning and say 'I know that Eddie Irvine is a bit of a lad, it's time we did something on him, what can I invent that sounds really wacky and will make the editor take notice of me?'

ANOUK

As you've heard, it didn't start very well as I thought we were going to spend the weekend with Eddie Jordan and that wasn't really on my agenda. Finally, when I did meet up with him, I thought he was a little bit over the top. We went out to a bar and then later on to a club, but I really wasn't attracted to him at all. He was a good looking guy, and he got a lot of attention, and he was playing up to it, messing around. Later on that weekend, we had some good conversations and we really got on well. I started to see the man behind the mask. When we did start talking he was not really the same guy I met on that first night in Milan. It really got me interested. When I went back to New York he called me and I called him and it went from there. We've been together ever since.

He's two different people depending whether you're alone with him or in a group of people. I think he has to stick to a certain image when he's doing his job and has a lot of people around him. But when I spend time alone with him, he's very calm and a relaxed person to be with. He's very charismatic and I really enjoy being with him. I've always preferred it when someone's independent and has his own life. It's the same for me, I like to be independent and have my own interests. And then there's the sparkle in his eyes, which I find very attractive.

In the beginning a lot of people said to me 'Oh my god, why are you going out with this guy? He's a womaniser, there's a million women round him. Why don't you find someone who will be just with you rather than be one of hundreds who are crazy about him?' Of course he has a lot of attention, as I saw when I went on a promotion with him in Dublin, and women go crazy when they see him, but there's no point in getting upset. From the beginning I knew he was the centre of attention for a lot of women and that he was a bit of a sex symbol. I might not like it, but I can accept it or not. I can walk out or choose to stay, and I chose the latter. At the end of the day when women throw themselves at him, I just say to myself, you can flirt with him, talk to him, and do what you like, but he's going home with me tonight not with you.

I don't think he ever gets jealous of me, at least he never shows it. Sometimes I think it annoys him when I talk to certain men, but he's not really the jealous type. He's too independent to be jealous and he doesn't like thinking of people as possessions but as people with their own separate identities. As for me, there's no point in being jealous. If I started being jealous with Eddie Irvine there'd be no end to it. You could make it into your main occupation.

I went to a charity event with a photographer that I work with, and I heard him say to a girl 'This is Eddie Irvine's girlfriend.' She looked at me and it was as if fire came out of her eyes and she said 'I officially hate this girl right now!' I was very impressed. She meant it as a joke, but I could tell she was a little bit disappointed. It made me realise that Eddie is a big star. It was quite shocking really. I hadn't realised he caused such a fuss amongst the female population.

Sometimes it bothers me when he talks about ex-girlfriends. There are certain situations I don't need to know about, but if he's spent a couple of years with a couple of different girls then that's part of his life. We talk about his ex-girlfriends and my ex-boyfriends. Maybe we should hook them up together. Certain situations upset me a little bit, but I guess that's because I want to keep some things close to me. In the beginning it was quite a laugh when his friends talked about women and sex, but it got very boring. I'd just get up and walk off. I don't need to sit at a table with eight men hearing about what happened two years ago in Eddie's life. I know they're just joking and having a bit of fun, but a couple of times I got to the point when I felt enough was enough, and just walked out for a bit or screamed at the top of my lungs. Most of the time, though, his friends are nice and very laid back and fun.

Eddie is really fond of his friends, but he's not really an emotional guy. He doesn't show love and affection easily. We've talked about it and I think it's quite Irish not to show the depth of your feelings, especially when other people are around. It's much easier for me to be affectionate in company. Initially, when other people were around he wouldn't put his arm round me, seeming to think it wasn't macho, or would in some way demean his masculinity, but now he's much more affectionate. Maybe it just takes him a while to get to that stage.

He certainly showed trust in me very quickly and soon took me into his confidence about the team and what bothered him, but he's not emotional. It makes me smile now that on the first day I met him I said to him 'The only person I have heard of in motor racing is Schumacher.' Not the best thing to say on the first day! Although he and Schumacher work together and they both know it's better to have a good working relationship, I don't think they're personal friends. Although we don't discuss racing that much, every now and then we ask ourselves what it would be like if Eddie won the World Championship. I think it would be so incredible.

Eddie's been a little more relaxed since Schumacher is out of the frame, and it's a great opportunity for him to finally show what he can do. In Austria he was under a lot of pressure as some people were saying he was all talk, but Eddie is the kind of guy who thrives on that sort of thing and he showed them and won. I was watching the race in Holland, and they were saying that he always has a big mouth but he still does it. I was laughing because that's the way he is.

I've been to some of the races and at the beginning of the race I'm always a little scared because there are so many cars so close together. I don't really know the sport well enough to know what's happening and I don't think it is actually possible to be really relaxed if somebody you love participates in a high risk sport.

Silverstone was a heart-stopping moment. I saw two red cars getting really close and then one went off. I had no clue who it was as you cannot really tell the difference. It was about five seconds before they showed on the screen that it was Michael and not Eddie who had gone off. Those were the longest five seconds I've ever known. But I know he is confident doing his job. He doesn't joke around with it, and he knows what he's doing, so I trust him.

We've had some great times together. I've spent time with him on his boat, where he taught me to jet-ski, which was great as he really took time and trouble to make sure I got it right, and he's been to New York to see me, before the race in Montreal. When he came to New York I realised that he really felt relaxed with me when we were spending time together, and I realised that a lot had happened in a short time.

I have been to Northern Ireland to his home and met his parents. I was a bit worried about it as I thought they must think, 'Here's model number 43 and this time she's blonde. Here's another chick hang-ing around with him because she likes the image and the world he's living in.' I hope they've changed their minds a bit by now. I really love being with him and I'm in love with him. I wouldn't be spending as much time as possible with him if I wasn't. He's a real per-son, very down to earth, and I think that's quite hard to find in someone who is a star. If you're in that posi-tion you can lose your head. But I think that no matter what happens he'll always be the same guy.

EDDIE: My first girlfriend was Lesley McKenzie, we went to the same swimming club. I must have been eleven or twelve, something like that, and I've never looked back. Once I'd discovered girls then it was all systems go, they were more fun than homework and a lot more fun than anything I'd come across before. People accuse me of being a 'love them and leave them' type, but I don't leave them, I let them catch me out and then leave me. That happened with Monica, the girl I went out with before Anouk. I told her I was in Corsica, and then she came cruising past the boat on another boat outside Portofino. I had three topless women on top of the boat, and I was on my jet-ski. I actually hadn't done anything, but the evidence was overwhelming, so that ended that romance. But she's still a really good friend. We had dinner in Milan in September, and we had a laugh.

I keep in touch with a lot of my ex-girlfriends. After all, I went out with them because I really like them not because I just wanted to screw them. People think it's all about sex, but it's as much about liking them and getting on with them, and having a good laugh. I don't fall out with my girlfriends. I was out with Nicola in the summer and she is a girlfriend from a few years back.

There is one, though, who doesn't speak to me and that's Yvonne Connolly, who's now married to Ronan Keating. There was a lot of talk about her child being mine, but that was just rubbish. Yvonne and I had a fling well before she married Ronan. Yvonne is very photogenic, but it was never destined to be a big love job. For a start I was seeing someone else at the time, and so I only saw her whenever I was back in Dublin. It just didn't feel right for many reasons which I don't want to go into. I think it is enough to say it didn't work and she went off and married Ronan, and I'm happy for her.

The night I met her, I was with my mate, The Doc. He and I went to an international models' do at The Point in Dublin. We were in the front row with all the glitterati behind us, and afterwards we went to P.O.D. nightclub, along with a number of models – Yasmin Le Bon, Karen Mulder, Naomi Campbell, Christy Turlington, and Yvonne. I was eyeing up Yvonne so The Doc went over to her and said 'Yvonne, I have a friend who fancies you,' and she said 'I know.'

'How do you know?'

'Well, he has been looking at me all night, hasn't he?'

Two days later we went down to a beach in Killeny Strand with a group of friends. The following day we went down to Cork to an Oasis concert, where we stayed with a friend and had a good laugh and all got on really well together. After that weekend Yvonne became a core member of our group until we had a great but slightly strained skiing holiday during the New Year of 1998 and on our return everyone just seemed to go their own way. To the surprise of all of us, a few months later Yvonne went off and married Ronan.

There have been rumours about me and David Coulthard's girlfriend, Heidi, but nothing doing there either. Heidi used to hang out with our group before going out with DC, but not with me. I don't really consider myself to be a playboy, to me a playboy is someone who lives off money they've never earned, someone who just plays. Well, that's not me. I know playboys who live off daddy's money and they're very one-dimensional. I play hard but work hard, too.

To be honest I haven't thought about what sex and love mean to me. I just have a good time and see where it leads me. All I know is that this is the best time of my life. I've been incredibly lucky, both in love and in life. For instance, I had to put all my eggs in one basket with the Honda thing, it's what I'd set my heart on, and they go and do the thing with BAR. Then Ford buy Stewart and I get to drive with Jaguar which is even better. It's the same with girls. I've met some wonderful girls and am having a great time. Sometimes I can't believe I'm so lucky.

But I did get into trouble for criticising a particular supermodel. I was with a journalist at the time and some very average looking girls. Thinking I'd try and be nice, I said something like 'Supermodels are not always stunning, you know. The most beautiful girls in the world don't always photograph well, and the most photogenic don't always look as great to me in real life.' I named an example and that was it. It hit the papers and now I don't suppose that one supermodel is my favourite fan. I wasn't really criticising her, just trying to be nice to these girls. Actually it is a fact that some of the supermodels look good in real life, while some really don't. Christy Turlington is beautiful in photographs and beautiful in real life, and in the flesh. I went out with Karen Mulder once in Paris and she's also very beautiful as well. We have several friends in common.

When you meet so many beautiful girls, beauty becomes less important. No matter how beautiful a girl is, after three or four weeks of being with her, she becomes ugly if she has an ugly personality. Anyway, to start with, my girl pulling isn't infallible. I have had some failures, but not many, not because I'm the greatest, but because I usually get a vibe from the girl before I make a move, so I try and limit the risk of rejection. If you just make a move without seeing how the land lies, then you risk failure; if you're cautious there's less chance.

The first time I had sex wasn't a great experience. I was 15 and it went on forever, I just kept on going and going. I don't think the earth moved for her, she just kept telling me to hurry up. She was a lot older than me and she was worried because we were in a car behind my grandmother's house. She was scared my grandmother would come out and find us. Meanwhile, I was just drilling away, and drilling away. Things have changed now. The setting might be a bit more luxurious and international, but I wish I could last that long! It's strange what life brings you, I could never imagine that I'd have the opportunity to meet and bed so many beautiful girls. It's like some wonderful dream. I don't know whether things will ever change, but I suppose they do. The fact that I've been faithful to Anouk for six months has to say something about me. I don't know what, as I haven't analysed it. I don't know whether it's time for fathers to celebrate and unlock all their daughters, or whether Anouk will get fed up, move on and leave me on the loose again.

CHAPTER 11

Monza & Nurburgring

I couldn't deal with the pre-Italian Grand Prix test at Monza every day of the week. I've never experienced anything like it. People were putting bits of paper in my face to sign constantly. I couldn't go to the toilet in peace. I'd be eating dinner and people would still be shoving pieces of paper in my face. Things on the track weren't much better. During the test I was half a second slower than Mika Salo, and I was pretty depressed about it. In addition, everyone was trying to tell me what to do, which I found incredible. I spent three days complaining about the car and it was only in the last hour that we changed the front wing, floor and rear wing, and it went the way I wanted it to go. Suddenly instead of 1 min 25.1, I'm doing 1 min 23.8 seconds, the quickest time of any team. But because we'd only made the changes in the last hour, it meant we had done all that testing with a car that was wrong so it was a wasted week.

It was also a strange kind of week as Ferrari chose to make the announcement that I would be leaving. There was a huge volume of press requests that then had to be handled. Enrico and I felt it would have been better left until after Monza, allowing us to concentrate on the matter in hand – fighting for the championship.

Luckily I was able to get away for a few days' break on the boat with my daughter Zoe, and my parents, Sonia and Maria. It was business combined with pleasure as Jez and Andy were filming for a documentary, and Jane was discussing this book with me. People ask me why I need to do all these things, but my attitude is that I have to earn as much as possible as when it ends, it ends. I don't do as much as I used to, and I'm more discerning. I now earn more for doing less, as my profile has increased. I feel in some ways it's more of a thrill to have £500 in your hand than one million in the bank. It is difficult to imagine one million pounds, but if you have cash in hand you can buy this or that.

I have a great life, and I wouldn't change it for anything. I remember when George Best had finished playing. He was in bed with Miss World in a hotel suite, and had just won money at the casino, and had covered the bed with notes. He ordered a bottle of champagne from room service and when the waiter came in he looked at Best and said 'Where did it all go wrong George?' George knew he meant his playing career, but he looked around the room, saw Miss World in bed, money all over the place and champagne and asked 'Has it all gone wrong?'

Monza is one of the hot races for famous faces. Sylvester Stallone comes every year, as do a lot of soccer stars and other VIPs. It's a very demanding few days, but the atmosphere at Monza is incredible. My main objective for this weekend was to beat Hakkinen, but if I couldn't do that, then I had to win points and keep close to him so I could continue the fight for the Championship. Everybody said Spa was a disaster but I came out of it with three points, and so I felt it was a success for me.

Unfortunately the whole Monza weekend was difficult from our point of view. On the Friday we concentrated on the race programme, working on different fuel loads. I tried different set ups but didn't manage to find one that suited me. It seemed that the track was more slippery than the week before. I thought that after studying the data, and working on qualifying, we would have managed to do a lot better than our actual qualifying positions, which were disastrous.

Hakkinen was on pole, not a big surprise. Frentzen managed to split the McLarens, and push Coulthard to third with Zanardi fourth and Ralf Schumacher fifth. Mika was sixth, followed by Rubens Barrichello and I was in eighth, not very impressive when you consider the amount of testing we do, and also that there were so many teams ahead of us. Williams has been coming up and getting better every race. I think Ralf is a bit of a revelation this year, he's got his act together and is doing a good job for Williams. Jordan have also got very strong in the last few races. The basic problem at Ferrari is that we just hadn't made enough progress with the car over the last three or four races. We had some things on line for Nurburgring, but that wasn't helping us now, and the fans weren't impressed.

I got held up by a yellow flag on my last run, but it wouldn't have affected my time very much. More important for this circuit was to improve the aerodynamics. At least we had a new version of the engine, which was a step in the right direction. At that point on Saturday I thought my best chance in the race was to make a great start. My aim was to get as many points as possible and I thought Frentzen could help us by getting in the midst of the McLarens, who are our main rivals.

On the Saturday night we had a couple of Philip Morris promotion events to go to, including a dinner with Ferrari Chairman Luca di Montezemolo, which had all the press guys there as well. We get used to it but at Monza there's always a lot of promotions stuff to do. After that there was the Candy dinner, at which I made an appearance. It was the usual thing – turning up, a few questions asked by the

Italian TV journalist, Claudia Peroni, and signing autographs. Finally, at the end of a long day, I went back to the flat in Milan on the scooter. Scooters are the only way to get in and out of Monza. If you take the car you just sit there for hours. I was knackered when I got back but did not sleep all that brilliantly.

I woke up on race day feeling quite flat. I sensed that things were pretty much out of my hands and that my position in the World Championship after Monza would depend on other drivers committing errors. I don't like that, I like to be in control, knowing what I can do to change things. In addition to our poor grid positions, we had to deal with the chaos that always surrounds Monza – endless visits to the garage, and politicians getting in on the act. It's constant distraction when you need to get down and focus on the job in hand.

ENRICO

I think Eddie was very frustrated by the situation at Monza. The car was just not performing as it should have been at this point in the Championship and Eddie was powerless to do anything about it. That is very difficult for him as he is the driver, responsible for the result. He gets the glory when he wins a race, but he has to take the flak even when he can't do much about it. It's also difficult for me to patch everything up and keep everything going.

I never enjoy race day, it's the worst day of the week. Sonia and I try to ensure he has minimum pressure in relation to outside activities and press interviews. It was hard working with the sponsors at

Monza, though if he'd been in pole position it would have probably been different, he would have been able to have a chat and a laugh with some of the sponsors, but as the car was performing so badly he just wanted to run away.

Sonia

I knew Eddie was feeling frustrated about his grid position, but I was confident he'd turn it round in his head and make it work for him. That's one of his strong points, he can always think positive and put things in a good light, which is exactly what he needed to do at this race.

The morning of the race followed our usual routine. I made him breakfast and then for me it was a case of getting the drinks and food ready for after the race, checking on the sponsors and guests, sorting out his post-race gear, and generally making sure that every-thing happened when it should.

The race was a disaster for Ferrari, but fortunately it was a bigger disaster for McLaren. I didn't know it at the time but Hakkinen made a driver error and went off. I thought the car had broken down or something, but to repeat the mistake of Imola was just incredible. It would be nice for us if he could make it a hat trick, possibly at the last race! On the other hand, neither was my race covered in glory. I was a bit too cautious at the start as I knew it was vital for me to finish the race, and thinking about it, I feel it might have been better to push, as that caution might have cost me one or two places. But then I could have pushed and had someone go into me, and gone off, and I wouldn't have got even one point.

Mika had a better day and finished on the podium so he experienced what it is like to be on the podium at Monza. It is a unique experience, but I wish it had been me. There wasn't any point in him lifting off to let me through, as he was in third and we had two cars between us. Coulthard was one of them and he could have picked up valuable points, which could have helped him and McLaren, so tactically there wasn't much to do about it.

It was embarrassing that Salo was ahead of me, especially it being Monza. But I felt he wasn't actually quicker than me, or as good technically, and when we tested after Monza the reasons why I had been slower during the race became clear and we made aerodynamic changes to rectify the situation. I think that having Michael's input at this point would have helped. The two of us have worked together for many years, and we've got our own ideas, and together we can come up with a solution, and we've lost that chance at the moment. Mika is good but we haven't been working together for very long.

The changes we made to the car meant it was quicker in terms of top speed, but it was bad on kerbs. Now at least we are away from these type of circuits, although I have to say I was a bit worried about the chicane at Nurburgring. It's important as that's where McLaren were good last year. They're good in the last sector, and we have to counter that and find something ourselves. At Monza we'd got out by the skin of our teeth. If Hakkinen hadn't lost it, then we would have been in deep shit. If he'd won I would have been nine points behind him, with only three races to go.

I thought that Nurburgring would be better for us as we had some aerodynamic changes that I thought would improve the performance of the car. I was optimistic about the weekend, but it all went horribly wrong. Due to the weather, qualifying was chaos, with most of the cars staying in the pits until the last twenty minutes. I went out as the track was drying and snatched the fastest time, before everyone came out and it was a case of who would be fastest when the session finished. As it turned out it was Frentzen with DC second and Hakkinen third. I felt I would have been good for a second row position, but I aborted my penultimate lap due to traffic. I didn't want to run into Panis on my last lap so I backed off. I knew that if I didn't get a good time I'd be nowhere as the track was drying out. I held back for the last lap and then locked my rear brakes on a damp patch, went onto the grass, and that was the end of that. I could have been on pole but ended up ninth, a disaster. We could have been kings now we were tossers. Once again, we could only hope that our main rivals, McLaren, would make a mistake.

I hadn't given up as the weather was uncertain and I thought we'd chosen the right tyres. We'd paid the penalty in qualifying of choosing hard tyres, but it should have been good for the race. The others would struggle on soft tyres for the first ten or fifteen laps, so it was our chance to put pressure on them. In a situation where you have changeable weather then it's usually down to the team with the best strategy and I have always thought Ferrari excelled in this area. I was hoping master strategist Ross Brawn could pull it off again.

However, things just didn't work out. Thankfully,

things also went wrong for McLaren. They pulled Hakkinen in to put on wet tyres when he was second behind Frentzen. It had only just started to rain and it stopped pretty much straightaway. Of course, they should have experimented with Coulthard first. Hakkinen then had to stop four laps later to put on dry tyres. We made a lot of decisions that seemed to be right at the time but during the race turned out to be wrong. We went for a three stop strategy, as we thought McLaren would be in trouble with their tyres at the beginning of the race, and we thought we could put pressure on them. But then the pace car came out and shot that strategy to pieces. We spent six laps cruising round not being able to overtake.

In the pit stop Mika came in as he had damaged his front wing. There was no other option because if it had fallen off it could have caused a big accident. It was just sod's law that he broke the wing two laps before I was due to come in. This meant that the crew were expecting me and had everything ready to change my tyres. So they put my tyres to one side and grabbed his. They put his tyres on and then went to get mine, but by this stage someone, who had just seen a tyre lying there unwrapped, had picked my tyre up and put the tyre blanket back on it and put it back on the shelf.

As well as this, we stayed out too long waiting for wets. It was my call. I'm supposed to come in when I want to change to wet tyres. Ross was saying 'Stay out, stay out,' and I should have overruled him. It's difficult to overrule someone as powerful as Ross, but I should have done, and I probably wasn't strong enough. Then I thought he was too late calling for slicks. It's my call to call for wets, his call to call for slicks as he can see the times of other people who have already gone to slicks. It was just a catalogue of small things that added up to a disaster. As soon as Ross saw we had screwed up on the pit stop, he thought 'Shit, we've really screwed up here, let's do damage limitation,' so he kept concentrating on Hakkinen, saying 'Hakkinen's right behind you with no problems, just keep going, we need to cover Hakkinen.' After the race, I said to him 'Forget about Hakkinen, they screwed up, we need to get points to win this Championship, there's no point in being safe all the time.'

I think he agreed with that after the race, but I think the pit stop really threw him, which is unusual. Not only is Ross very good, but he's usually very cool. We analysed it, discussed it and then put it to one side. You have to get on with the next race. I do remember , though, sitting in the car at the pit stop thinking 'Shit!' I'd made it up to fifth position and I thought I was still in with a chance. Hopefully it won't happen again. You can't really blame the pit crew – it was just a series of things that went wrong. It was just a nightmare of co-incidences.

I do think, however, that it is wrong having only one pit crew. Every team in Formula One should have two pit crews. That would make it much fairer, as the system we have always prejudices one driver. If I came in on a yellow flag, then I'd have to wait for them to re-fuel Michael. If I carried on round under a yellow flag then I lose time. It is a ridiculous system. Also it would make for a good competitive atmosphere within the team as each pit crew would try and outdo the other in terms of doing the best time and the most efficient pit stop.

In the end though in some strange way it seems like someone up there in heaven wants me to have a chance at this Championship. Michael's return is a great advantage, and will frighten McLaren for the next two races. Maybe it will be like Manchester United in the European Cup Final. They're losing one-nil, with the ninety minutes played, and then they score two in extra time. Their name was written on the Cup. I hope my name is written on the World Championship trophy. I think we've got a fair crack at it. I'm certainly hungry for it, but in some ways our destiny is slightly out of our hands, as it depends on McLaren as much as on us. For the last four years everyone has been expecting Michael Schumacher to take the title. It would be a wonderful story if I won for Ferrari, and Formula One is full of wonderful stories. Let's hope this one comes true.

Epilogue

● ●

A TRIP EAST

I had decided to take my plane to the Far East, and to stop off at various places on the way from Malaysia to Japan. My plane has a range of about 1500 nautical miles, so we could do the trip in three short legs, and also get acclimatised to the time difference in a leisurely way, rather than catching a commercial flight and being transported through several time zones in one go. My spin doctor Enrico re-invented it as the 'Marco Polo Tour', and Philip Morris asked if they could send a photographer along to take some photos and do a daily bulletin on the trip.

We all set off from Bologna on the afternoon of the 7 October, and landed in Cairo in the evening. By lunchtime the next day we were standing staring at the Pyramids and the Sphinx. I was deeply impressed by the scale of it all – the pyramids were a lot bigger than I thought they would be. The engineering skills of the people who built them were extraordinarily advanced. I think that after the building of the Pyramids, civilisation definitely took a step backwards. It's taken us a long time to catch up (if we ever really have).

The next stop was Dubai and we reached the air-conditioned coolness of our 6-star hotel in the middle of a boiling afternoon. We had arranged to meet up with some friends who live in there. I had met them in St. Tropez, and they put on a very special evening for Enrico and me. Everything was organised to perfection, from the champagne and food to the entertainment.

It was, however, incredibly hot in Dubai with humidity running at about 88%. I really hoped it wasn't going to be like that in Kuala Lumpur. That evening I'd been for a run and found it took a lot more effort than normal to cover my usual distance. It isn't the heat that knackers you so much as the humidity. It's essential to watch out for dehydration and keep your fluid intake up. If it was going to be like that in Kuala Lumpur then my diet, and above all my liquid intake, would have to be seriously revised.

The next afternoon we took off for New Delhi. We arrived around midnight and headed straight to the Sheraton for a welcome night's rest. The next morning we had a short tour of the city, which I found very green and very peaceful. I was expecting it to be much more chaotic than it was. Sure, there was some heavy traffic, but nothing like the mayhem I'd been led to expect. I was also booked in for some promotional work, which involved a ride on an elephant. That was a bit different. It was certainly an experience but I don't think I'll be taking it up as a full-time job. The vehicle might be bigger, greyer and slower but sitting on top of an elephant feels a lot more unstable than driving a Formula One car.

The last leg of our journey was to Phuket via Calcutta. We spent three nights in Phuket at the Lagoona Beach, and that was when I really had a chance to catch up on my sleep and just relax and chill out. The people there are fantastic, they smile all the time. In Europe I'm used to people smiling at me and being nice to me and ignoring my friends, as I'm famous and they're not. But in Phuket they were smiling at everyone, and they hadn't a clue who I was, so it was totally genuine. It's a place I'd definitely go back to. People say I'm difficult to get close to and talk to, but I don't like false people, the type who will be nice to you only because they think they should. I'll talk to people who I think are good inside, and there were a lot of genuine people in Phuket. The food is fantastic as well. Thai food is one of my favourite foods, and so it was a chance to eat well, sleep, read, do some training on the beach and play a little tennis. It was very, very quiet and a great place to be before going into the chaos that would be Malaysia.

We arrived in Kuala Lumpur on Wednesday 13 October and headed straight into a press conference with Michael. Obviously, I knew Michael was coming back – whether he had decided to come back or had been asked, I didn't know and didn't particularly care. The main question in many people's minds was how much Michael's come back was going to be able to help the team. I'd certainly helped him during the last four years.

To be quite honest, I felt like it didn't really affect me whether Michael's return was successful or not. From the point of view of set up, I'd done my own thing for a couple of years, so I wasn't relying on him from a technical point of view. I rely on my mechanics and my team and I know I can rely on Ross Brawn, but I don't take any notice of the political intrigue which can sometimes surround a major team like Ferrari.

However, that doesn't mean I wasn't pleased to see Michael back in the fold. We've been team mates for nearly four years, and to have a strong team mate means we have an extra option and someone who understands the situation with our competitors. Mika Salo was great and I don't want to take anything away from what he did for us – he came in, put in a huge effort and did brilliantly – but I did think that Michael's presence could help us a lot regarding the situation with McLaren. They would now have to deal with Michael's forceful presence in the team, which meant they would have to develop a different strategy towards the race. Niki Lauda thought that Michael could unsettle Mika Hakkinen, which would be valuable for us. At this stage in the game we needed every advantage we could muster, and a psychological advantage is always positive. However no one had taken the decision about what our strategy was going to be, and I think the press had had enough with the uncertainty in the air. For my part, I had to just concentrate on my main aim of the weekend – to take the title to Suzuka, and fight it out to the bitter end.

It's pretty rare to have a new venue in Formula One. In the past twenty-five years we've only added Japan, Australia and Hungary to the calendar, although there have been occasions when we've returned to countries that hosted grands prix many years ago. The circuit at Sepang in Malaysia is very tough, but it's a great track. It's taken them more than two years to build, and they've done a good job. There are many different types of corner – fast ones, blind ones, long ones – and this adds up to three first/second gear corners, four third gear, four fourth gear and two fifth gear turns. It throws down a great challenge to the drivers, who find a combination of everything on the track. It might seem easy at first glance, but the track narrows at certain points and the camber changes, so making it much more difficult.

It isn't easy to get the best set up as you have to calculate optimum downforce. We reckoned it would be in the medium range, like Silverstone, as opposed to low downforce, high speed circuits like Monza or Hockenheim, or high downforce, low speed circuits like Monaco. In addition, tyre grip is vital and we knew that tyre choice would be critical here. Overtaking is very hard in Formula One, but I thought the main straight and the following Turns 1 and 2, which are fairly tight but with high positive cambers, should provide good overtaking opportunities.

We had done our homework before going out to the race and these days, with modern technology at our fingertips, it isn't that difficult to get to know a new circuit fairly quickly. We had made some changes for Nurburgring and aerodynamically made a good step forward. We had had a new floor for Nurburgring as well, although what with everything else that happened at the race, our improvements had not been obvious for anyone to see. Nevertheless, I was convinced that we'd progressed technically at Nurburgring, and that we were set up for a good performance in Malaysia. The best scenario we could have hoped for was to get both cars on the front row, make a great start, and leave the McLarens to chase us. Happily, that's more or less what happened.

Michael got pole with a blinding 1m 39.688 sec. The rest of us were quite knackered at this point in the season, but Michael came back after three months rest and just blasted us into orbit. No one had expected the times to go below 1m 40 secs, but he was nearly a second ahead of me in second place with 1m 40.635 sec. With fifteen minutes to go the McLarens had briefly split Michael and me with Hakkinen going second, but I had managed to get back on the front row again. DC made my day when he snatched third place from Mika Hakkinen who ended up fourth on the grid.

It was great to get front row of the grid and it put us in the right position for the start, but we've learnt that the race can be a different thing altogether. I won in both Austria and Germany from further back on the grid, so you never know what can happen.

We had a two stop strategy with the option of one stop if we felt it was necessary. Some people have criticised Ferrari's team tactics, but they forget that this is a team sport. Two drivers compete for the Constructors' Championship, so I don't see the problem with the team employing tactics that will help them win that trophy, while also going for the Drivers' Championship. On this occasion, though, my impression was that it was only decided just before the race that the team would really go for the Drivers' as well as the Constructors' Championship. I didn't let the uncertainty bother me. I knew what I intended to do, and so I just followed that plan and let everyone sort themselves out.

Michael did the perfect job for me during the race. I couldn't have asked for a better wing man. He's a great number one, but an amazing number two! I wonder what it would take to get him to cover for me at Jaguar? Michael let me through on lap 4, and then he set about keeping Mika Hakkinen at bay. The one thing we hadn't reckoned

on was DC's enthusiastic move on Michael, when he overtook him at Turn 2. That threatened to turn the race around
as DC was quicker than me. I found the tyres were difficult
in the first few laps, and so I couldn't push as hard as I
would have liked. Fortunately, luck was on our side and
DC ground to a halt on lap 15.

Once DC was out of the game, then it was down to us.
Michael kept Mika Hakkinen back while I built up a lead.
McLaren went for hard tyres and I don't think that was his
best choice. After his second pit stop Hakkinen was behind
Johnny Herbert and that would have been ideal for us. If
Mika had finished in fourth he would have scored three
points instead of four for third, and that would have meant
I could beat him in Japan if he won and I came second. But
Johnny ran wide and Hakkinen went through.

I chose to put scrubbed tyres on for my second pit stop
as they felt better. It all went totally to plan and Michael let
me through and I won with Michael second and Hakkinen
third. It was just what I wanted and it took it all to Japan. I
think the result was good for everyone. Michael had been
fantastic and I couldn't have asked for him to do more. He
not only let me through, but protected my position by driving carefully and keeping Hakkinen behind him. But his
speed when he built up some time before his pit stop, and
just before he let me through to win the race, proved once
again that he is an awesome driver. His performance had
proved he's the best driver, so he was happy. I was also
very happy that I still had a chance to go for the
Championship and Ferrari were happy to be leading both
the Drivers' and the Constructors' Championships. We all
felt it couldn't be more perfect.

In fantastic spirits I left for the airport where my plane was waiting, and Enrico and I prepared to go to Macau for a few days to see Maria and Zoe. I was on top of the world. It's funny how you can go from hero to zero in a few hours.

Just as we'd arrived at the airport, I got the call from Jean Todt. 'We have a problem,' he said.

ENRICO

We were both really happy about the race, it had gone exactly as we had hoped. Michael had done a fantastic job and helped Eddie, which I was particularly pleased about as Eddie has helped him in the past, and it was good to see teamwork at its best. Michael also proved by the way he drove during the race that he's the best driver and so he must have been satisfied, and Eddie was leading the Drivers' Championship.

Eddie got a phone call at the airport, but I didn't think he was talking to Jean Todt. In fact, there was nothing about his demeanour to suggest anything was wrong. I thought it had just been a friend calling him. When we took off, though, he said 'That was Jean Todt, something's wrong.' I said 'Don't worry, it's probably nothing.' I just didn't imagine anything was really wrong.

But he said 'I think there is something wrong.' So we had a bet. We always bet a pizza, and this time I lost, which is really unusual as I normally win. I bet him that Ferrari wouldn't be disqualified. We landed in Bangkok to re-fuel and I spoke to Jean Todt and Eddie spoke to Ross Brawn. They confirmed in detail what had gone wrong. It turned out the barge boards were illegal by 1cm. The rules are too complicated to go into the detail of why, but apparently McLaren had complained and the FIA technical delegate Joe Bauer had measured the parts and found they didn't comply with the rules and were 10mm or 1cm out.

We spent the rest of the journey to Macau analysing and discussing what had gone wrong, and what would happen. We rang a few people and stayed in touch with Ferrari, speaking to Jean Todt on a daily basis. Everyone was very depressed. Even at Ferrari the reaction was very negative, people were very down and thought that that was it for the season. We weren't. We had the attitude of, 'Well, we'll just have to wait and see.'

We landed in Macau and Eddie spent three or four days with Maria and Zoe, his daughter, which was the best thing he could have done. It was the first time I had the opportunity to observe him as a family man, and it was quite a revelation. Here's this single guy, the ultimate playboy, who loves women and knows how to party and enjoy life to the full, in other words the last man you'd expect to be good at playing happy families, and yet here he is slipping happily into the role of father.

Being a father obviously comes naturally to him, and he loved being with Zoe. He just played with her solidly for four days. As well as being his manager, I also like Eddie and if he's happy, then I'm happy, and I saw him very happy as part of a family. Maria is a great girl, she has known Eddie very well for a long time and knows exactly how to handle him. If you bother him or hassle him he doesn't like you. As I've got to know him I've learnt not to keep on at him, but to give him his space and let him come to me. I don't call him – if he wants me, he will call me. Maria knows this and that makes them very comfortable together as friends and as parents.

I spent quite a lot of time with them – they'd come to the hotel swimming pool and I'd be there and join in and eat or swim. He went shopping with Maria for furniture for her new flat. Eddie and I played golf and it was really relaxing, just what he needed with all the trauma and confusion that was going on back in Italy. He didn't need to be in the middle of all that.

As Friday and the day of the appeal got nearer, we got a series of messages from Jean Todt, who was trying to get in touch with Eddie. He wanted Eddie to go to Paris for the hearing and Eddie himself wanted to be there and know what was going on. He felt impotent as the World Championship was in the hands of Ferrari and a panel of judges appointed by the FIA to preside over the appeal and make the final decision. The only thing he could do was to go to Paris to give moral support to the team. I think that shows how much of a team player he is. It took 36 hours; 12 hours on Air France to Paris, 12 hours in Paris and then 12 hours on Japan Airlines to Tokyo, but I think he showed the reality of who he is in that 36 hours. The team needed him and he was there. You can't ask for more than that from a driver.

I usually rely on gut instinct to tell me when something is amiss and I just didn't get that pit-in-the-stomach-feeling that it was all going to go horribly wrong. Other people were very depressed and down, but Enrico and I were reasonably cheerful. I couldn't see any reason to throw up my hands and fall into a depression. There was nothing I could do except wait and see what the judges decided. Personally I don't think it should ever have come to that in the first place. It seemed to me a case of being too hasty. Apart from anything else, if, as reported, the part was illegal and had been spotted at Nurburgring then why had they waited until after the race before lodging a protest, or measuring it? It all seemed a bit odd to me. I thought that to protest after the race was unfortunate. We well and truly kicked McLaren's arse in Malaysia and it seemed to me they didn't like it.

I decided to fly to Paris as I wanted to be with the team, and they wanted me there. As I flew back to Europe I could only hope that common sense would prevail. If the disqualification had held, Formula One would become like boxing and lose all credibility. You have to think of the sport and if everything descends into farce then you lose a lot of support. Bernie hadn't been present in Malaysia but had made it clear publicly that he wasn't happy.

I arrived in Paris at six in the morning and met up with Jean and Ross and the lawyers. Then we sat and waited and waited ... and waited. I positioned myself outside the courtroom, if you can call it that, and ate sandwiches while the others were presenting the case for Ferrari. Ross explained that they'd gone back to Maranello and measured the barge boards and then studied the rules and regulations, and that they believed that they were within the rules. The rules are so complicated now that I think it is difficult to be 100% certain if you're in or out. You have to remember that we're talking about millimetres and centimetres here. I've worked with Ross and Rory for several years now, and I can definitely say they are not cheats. If we had been outside the legal limits, it definitely wouldn't have been done deliberately. It just doesn't make sense to race with an illegal car. There's too much to lose and therefore no one plays that game, which is why I thought it was badly handled in Malaysia.

Eventually I was called in and the judges asked me a couple of questions as to whether it was usual for the team to protest after the race, and I explained that protests were usually made on the Thursday before the race, when scrutineering takes place. Jean was very nervous and I couldn't blame him, it was his neck on the line. As I've said before he has an impossible job; something goes wrong, and it's his fault, something goes well and it's the team who get the praise. Our lawyers, led by Henry Peter, thought the hearing had gone well, but I wasn't going to count my chickens. I remember appealing against my one race ban in 1994 and ending up with a three race ban. So I didn't have good memories about FIA hearings.

I flew back to Tokyo and waited for the result. As Jean Todt called me, I was watching Max Mosley on CNN giving his press statement. It was a huge relief and justice had been done. The part in dispute had been proved to be legal. That means that there is no question about legality. The car was legal and the World Championship would be clean. Enrico and I went out and celebrated in Tokyo.

Whatever happened on Sunday would be fair and square. I was going to go all out to clinch the Drivers' Championship and realise my dream.

I didn't think for one minute that this business in Paris had disrupted the team's preparation for Suzuka. They were 100% concentrated on the race, and we would all be giving it everything we had. With Michael helping us I felt that we had a 50/50 chance. The simple truth was if Hakkinen won, we'd blown it, if we won, we'd got it. Although the four point advantage was a good thing to have in the psychological battle, I felt pretty level-headed about it all. It could go either way and I knew it.

MARCUS PEKELER

I first met Eddie two years ago in St Tropez. I was with this girl on the beach, who was very pretty and we were having a great time. Then she said 'I have to meet this guy at three this afternoon.' So I said 'Okay, okay, let's go and meet him.' She said, 'I think his name is Eddie Irvine.' At this point I thought someone was taking the micky, and winding her up. I didn't think the real Eddie Irvine would show up. She hadn't a clue who he was, but about five minutes after this, Eddie showed up with Ciro. They were waiting for some other guys and we all sat around in the harbour and got drunk, and at about midnight the other guys turned up, and Eddie ended up with my girl on his boat!

But in spite of this he has become one of my closest friends. I have three or four really close friends and he's one of them. He's very natural and very normal, not at all spoiled by things. Most of my friends are like this as I don't like people who become famous and think they're something special, and start pushing people around and acting in an arrogant way. He just says what he thinks and I really like that about someone. Honesty is a good quality, especially in a friend. Eddie has a lot of friends from before he was famous, and I think that's very good. His cousins in Ireland are fantastic, it's like being part of a big family. If you belong to the family you're accepted and they take you to their hearts.

When Eddie's not racing I will often see him at weekends and we hang out in Milan or meet up in Paris or Dublin or wherever he happens to be. We shared an apartment in Milan. It was a tiny place and he would sleep on the sofa and I'd sleep in the bed. Then we decided to get something bigger, so we gave Ciro the job of finding a bigger apartment, which he did. Ciro looks after things when we're out of town, but he is the laziest housekeeper ever. A great guy but not the best housekeeper. Eddie is messy so it doesn't bother him that much, but I like to keep things in order. I think Ciro is the stereotypical chauvinist male. He relaxes and drinks beer while his girlfriend is slaving over a hot stove cooking dinner or washing up. Maybe he's got things right in life.

I've had some very funny times with Eddie. He said to me about a year ago, 'What are you doing on Saturday?' so I said, 'Nothing,' and he said 'Okay, let's go to Monte Carlo.' We took my car, arrived at the hotel in the evening, had a sleep and went out to din-

ner and onto Jimmy'z. The last time we'd been to
Jimmy'z we had problems getting in, so this time I
called them, and said 'I want to book your best table
for about one o'clock.' They were very obliging and
said, 'Yeah, okay, no problem.' When we got there after
dinner we realised why it had been so easy to book a
table. It had nothing to do with Eddie's name, the
place was totally empty. That's November in Monte
Carlo for you.

At about 2am Eddie said, 'Let's go home.' I thought
he meant back to the hotel, but he meant back to
Milan. I said 'You must be joking, it's a good two and
a half hour drive and that will be pushing it.' He said
'I'll drive. We're going to Milan.' So off we set. An
hour and a half later we were in a night club in Milan.
I have a racing Porsche and even I didn't know my car
could go that fast. Everyone was very surprised to see
us in the club, 'But I thought you were in Monte
Carlo,' they said. 'We were,' we said.

The only advice I can give to his male friends is if
you're in love with a beautiful girl then keep her away
from Eddie. I went to Paris earlier this year, and Eddie
said, 'You must call my friend Una, she's an American
model, and has loads of friends and is a great laugh.'
So I called Una and invited her over. She said 'I'd love
to come but I've got a friend of mine here and she's a
bit down as she's having problems with her
boyfriend.' So I said, 'Bring her over and I'll cheer her
up. The friend was Anouk. We all went out to a nightclub and got drunk and had a great time. We left the
club at six in the morning and Anouk went back to

New York shortly after that. I started calling her a lot and she came back to Europe, and Una bought her down to Milan. Eddie and I were sitting in this bar waiting for Una and Anouk to turn up. By this time I couldn't even remember what she looked like.

They were late and Eddie said 'Okay, let's go, they're late. I'm not hanging around.' I said to him, 'No, no, you've got to wait,' when all of a sudden Eddie started to look nervous. He was digging me in the ribs with his elbow, saying, 'Don't look now, but there's a fantastic girl coming down the stairs.' I looked and he nudged me again and said, 'Don't look, she'll think we're staring at her.' But then, of course, Anouk came straight up to me and said hello. Eddie was totally speechless. He said to me, incredulous, 'How could you forget what she looked like?'

The next day we left for his boat. I drove Anouk and Una and he drove various other girls down. He got rid of his current girlfriend, or at least she got rid of him after discovering him on his boat with five topless women! Then he concentrated on chatting up Anouk. I complained mildly to him that he was treading on my territory, but he just said to me, 'Marcus, don't try and eat steak in the lion's den.' So that was that. He started going out with Anouk shortly after that and has been seeing her ever since.

Eddie is very much the same at grands prix as he is in private, except he is naturally much more focussed at the track. Some people think that he doesn't take driving seriously, but he truly does. In Milan we'll go jogging for an hour a day, and although we'll have a laugh, he is very focussed. Things just seem to come together for him; he's had a fantastic career so far, and he certainly seems to have the luck of the Irish. When he won the race at Hockenheim, we were all down in the south of France waiting for him to arrive. When he turned up he sat down and said simply, 'I don't know what happened, but someone up there likes me.' His song is 'Lucky Man', and he's dead right, win or lose, he's still the Lucky Man. He's had experiences in life that are unique, and he's had intense emotions that many people never get to feel. He has lived his life to the full, and you can't do more than that.

I arrived in Tokyo a week early as it gave me a chance to concentrate on the week ahead and catch up with some of the friends I still have out there. I had some good times racing in F300 in Japan and I know my way round the city, so I always enjoy being back. It seemed very fitting that the next week in this city would decide whether or not I would be the 1999 World Champion.

The Title Fight

I always feel at home in Japan. I drove in my first grand prix here for Jordan in 1993, and it was also in Japan where I won my first World Championship points. It's like playing at your home stadium – I know the restaurants, the nightclubs, the bars, and the people and how they think.

Most of my old friends like James, Charlie Campbell, Philip the Fish, and Marcus couldn't make it to Japan. They had business commitments and also I wanted to be on my own to concentrate, but I was really pleased that one of my oldest supporters, Doctor Lanfranchi from Lampo, a company that make zips, flew all the way from Italy to Japan just for the race.

A couple of my Japanese friends, Shiga and Bobby, came along and of course Sonia was with me, as were my parents who were on their world trip exploring places they wanted to see.

James Bowles

I met Eddie about six years ago. We were in the same club, and I was with some girls, so we joined up and got on well. After that we'd meet up and play golf or go out to the local Italian restaurant for a pasta. He's good company and his close friends are a tight band who get on well together and have a good laugh.

Many years ago we were in Argentina for the grand prix. I was sharing a room with Eddie at the Alvear Palace, which is in the centre of Buenos Aires. Anyway, after the race me, Irv and Martin Brundle were having a chat, and DC came by and asked us what we were doing that night. We said we were just going out for a meal, then Mika Salo came by and joined up with us. We all went off to the Hard Rock Cafe, which was opposite the hotel, and while we were eating in came two stunning looking Argentinian girls. One of them decided to go for DC, and everyone tagged along to a few clubs and bars, before heading back to the hotel. It didn't work out for this girl with DC, and the last we saw of her she was disappearing in the hotel lift with Mika Salo.

Irv and I headed off to the Black Cat nightclub, which was supposed to be one of the 'in' places. We soon found out why. We arrived and the manager took us to one side and said 'Let me show you round my establishment.' We thought 'This is odd, it's only a nightclub.' Next thing we were walking through a hidden door in the room, and down a secret passage – all very James Bond – then we came to a wall and looked through a pin hole, through which we could see a room with a big round bed and a couple humping for Argentina. It was obviously a nightclub with a few extras, so we beat a hasty retreat back to the hotel.

By the time we got back to the hotel we were in a pretty happy state, so we decided to start on the practical jokes. I went to Reception and said my key card didn't appear to work. They asked me my name and I said 'Mr Salo.' They tried the key card and said that it must have the incorrect code, and gave me a new one. Irv and I then stormed into room 441 to find Mika Salo with the lovely Argentinian. He was a bit surprised to see us and suggested we should leave! But we sat down, raided his mini-bar and said that he should just ignore us. Then we pelted him with peanuts and left him to it.

He bought his boat just before the Monaco Grand Prix in 1998, and asked me to go down and look after it while he was racing. I didn't see Eddie as he was racing but we met up afterwards in the bar of the Hotel de Paris. Irv was mobbed as soon as he walked in so we headed for the Stars and Bars, and had a few drinks there. We wandered out of there and a big white limo pulled up, and Mick Hucknall called us over, so we all piled in and went off to Jimmy'z night-club. I thought it was all great, free flights, free accommodation, passes to watch the Grand Prix. I felt I'd really scored big time, so I decided to buy a round of drinks. We had four bottles of Dom Perignon champagne and the bill came to £1,240. So much for a cheap weekend!

Life is certainly full of surprises with Irv. We all got together last New Year's Eve. There was me, Irv, John Foley, Philip the Fish, Ronan, Champagne Charlie, Harry from Oakley Sunglasses, Cooperman and the loyal Charlie Campbell. We got a white stretch limo to Lily's Bordello, and hung around in the Library, with our American friend Jetboy buying everyone Cristal Champagne to drink. About £700 later we left out of the back door in the back of Ronan's van to go to Lisa Stansfield's party. It was a great night, a real giggle, and Irv ended up playing the guitar at Lisa's house.

We've decided that we'll do the same to celebrate the Millennium.

We've had some great times in Dublin. Once, we staggered out of one bar and found a guy with a rickshaw and so we got four of us on it. Me cycling, the guy who owned it pushing it, Ciro, Lord Harwood and Irv in the back. We set off for Reynards, down St. Stephen's Street passed a gawping queue at the taxi rank, into Grafton Street, clipping a few wingmirrors and went right bang slap into an Italian television crew, who didn't even recognise Irv! Once in Reynards, we pulled a couple of girls and wandered out. Then we noticed Cameron Diaz, so by this time fuelled by courage, I made a complete idiot of myself by going up to her and saying 'You're my best friend's best friend's best friend.' (She'd just been in *My Best Friend's Wedding*.) Unsurprisingly, we left shortly after that.

One of my best memories of Eddie is from last year when we went on a week's holiday together. At the beginning of December 1998 Eddie rang me and said 'What are you doing?' I replied 'Nothing much.' In fact, I had some holiday and so we agreed to meet the following week and he said 'Bring your passport and we'll go off for a week.'

I met him in London where he was involved in a discussion about die-cast models, then we took the train to Biggin Hill to meet up with the plane. The next day we flew over to Belfast and Eddie's dad met us and we spent a couple of days in Northern Ireland on a kind of pub crawl with a load of his friends. After this we made a brief stop at Farnborough on our way to Milan to look at a Ferrari Daytona that one of his friends had found him. He took it for a spin out of the airfield and then came back grinning like a Cheshire Cat, saying 'Yeah, I've bought it.' So now there was a Ferrari Daytona to add to the collection. Then we climbed back on board the jet and headed to Milan to meet up with his then girlfriend Monica, and his friend Marcus.

Marcus was feeling a bit put out as he'd bought an incredibly expensive pair of shoes for a model he was chasing, only to be outbid by a rich Arab who'd turned up with an expensive necklace. The necklace had won over the shoes, but we all killed ourselves laughing imagining the Arab out with this girl wearing Marcus's shoes! He didn't share our sense of humour over this. Still, it will teach him to go into an auction against a rich middle eastern gentleman, who was obviously loaded and hungry for the stunning girl.

We went on to a club called Hollywood and then had to drag ourselves out of bed at 6am to drive to Bologna where Eddie was doing a promotional appearance at the Bologna Motor Show. We got back about 11 pm, and I drove from Bologna to Milan, missing the turning of course! The next day I went out and about in Milan shopping and browsing around, while Irv stayed in the flat watching Eurosport.

Then we headed off to Jerez where he was supposed to be doing a three day test. We left Milan Malpensa Airport in the morning and it was freezing cold. We landed a couple of hours later in Jerez where

there was brilliant sunshine and blue skies. While
Eddie was testing, Alan Nee and I drove to Gibraltar
to deal with the boat.

We got back to Jerez to find that Michael had
turned up, to do the third day of the test. We then had
to decide what to do. I suggested we headed over to
Lisbon to stay at the Pennalonga hotel, which is a great
place on top of a hill overlooking the race track, and
with a golf course, too. This idea went down well so
Irv got out of the car, we got on the plane, flew to
Lisbon, drove to the hotel, checked in and were sitting
in the hotel bar drinking beer all within 44 minutes!
I thought I must get a private jet myself, it was just
fantastic. How else would you be able to fly from one
country to another, go from being in a Formula One
car to sitting in a bar in less than three quarters of an
hour. Now all I have to do is make the necessary
money!

Then it was time for me to make my way back to
cold old London. I was heading for Heathrow but Irv
asked me to go to City Airport and then pick up the
Daytona from the guy's showroom, and drive it to
Oxford. When I arrived it was still in the showroom so
they had to bring in the cranes to dismantle the front
of the building before I could get the car. Quite a
crowd had gathered by this time, and then I had to get
in and drive it. It is not an easy car to handle. By the
time I got back to Oxford I was exhausted after what
was supposed to have been a holiday. No wonder he's
knackered, that was just a week off for him, I felt like
I'd run the marathon. He then rang me up and asked

me to take the car to Ireland. I decided that was going a little too far and declined!

I have to say that Eddie's not changed much. His life is more demanding and he doesn't have very much time for a private life, but it won't always be like that, and I'm sure that once he retires he'll enjoy the toys and the lifestyle, turn into a successful business- man and play the stock market. But he'll always be an incredibly generous person.

Qualifying didn't go as well as I'd hoped. We didn't seem to be able to get the car right. I then had a fairly big shunt which gave me a sore neck during the race. Michael got pole and I thought we could still do it if Michael won. Then it would have been enough for me to come fourth to take the World Championship title, but it just wasn't to be.

I have to say that Mika drove a great race. On the day he was just the best, and I guess that if you look back over the year then we have both had our good and bad moments. You could say that if we hadn't cocked up at Nurburgring then we would have got at least two points and those two points could have won me the Championship. You could also say that if I hadn't given my place away in France we could have done it, but then Mika Hakkinen gave us plenty of chances as well by going into the wall at Imola and Monza. We both won and lost chances and in the end that is what it is about. You take your chances and you go for it, sometimes the dice lands your way, sometimes it doesn't.

When Michael didn't take the lead at the start I thought we were in trouble. Mika was just so quick it was obviously going to be very difficult for Michael to catch him. I just tootled around the circuit having a boring race and watching the television screens to see if Mika's car was going to give out any smoke signals, but it didn't. I don't think it's fair to expect your team-mate to win the World Championship for you, in the end it's down to you. On the day we just weren't up to it.

I did think that DC's move was a bit out of order. He was a lap down. He was under the blue flag and possibly lucky not to be penalised. Some people are asking if McLaren have made the right move in keeping DC for next year, but that's up to them. I'll be with Jaguar, and I'm looking forward to a new challenge.

In the circumstances it would have been very difficult to stay at Ferrari. I've had a bite at the title and I wouldn't have wanted to go back to the way things were before. Now I can join Jaguar and hopefully have another crack at the Championship. As I've found out this year, in this game you can never tell, and who knows where the dice will land next year. I hope that within the next few years my name will be written on the Drivers' Championship trophy, and then I'll have achieved my ultimate ambition.

Ferrari won the Constructors' Championship and I'm pleased I had an input in that. It means they get number one pit position next year which is a help, and it is an indication of great teamwork during 1999. There were a couple of instances where it didn't go according to plan, but in the main it was great teamwork all year. Ferrari have a great group of guys and I'll be sorry to see the end of my relationship with my team, but life moves on and I hope that success is just round the corner.

I start with Jaguar on 1 January. Until then I want to take a break see my friends and family, and just chill out. My idea of heaven is waking up with no schedule to keep to, no appointments, just the freedom to hop on the plane, or stay at home, go partying or stay in and watch the television.

Immediately after the Grand Prix I went to visit Maria and Zoe in Macau. I feel very comfortable with them, they are my family so it was the perfect place to go and be myself. Zoe just gets better and better every day and I want to spend more time with her in 2000. I just have to persuade Maria to move to Ireland, but it's a case of the rock meeting the immovable mountain, so we'll just have to see. I'd like them in Ireland as I'll be based in Europe. Now that I've left Ferrari I hope I can live in Italy with a little more freedom to move around without getting hassled.

It will take me a little while to digest this year, so near and yet so far, but after a few weeks holiday I'll get my head round it, pick myself up and carry on with life. As I've said before I'm a lucky man, I have a fantastic life, and I hope it's just going to get better and better.